THE HABSBURG EMPIRE

FRANZ HUBMANN

THE HABSBURG EMPIRE

THE WORLD OF THE AUSTRO-HUNGARIAN MONARCHY IN ORIGINAL PHOTOGRAPHS 1840—1916

EDITED BY ANDREW WHEATCROFT

NEW YORK
THE LIBRARY PRESS

CONTENTS

FOREWORD

This remarkable volume of photographs is the first visual history ever produced of the Austro-Hungarian Empire. It is a revised edition, with a new historical introduction by Andrew Wheatcroft, from the German edition entitled *K. u. K. Familienalbum*, published by Verlag Fritz Molden, Vienna 1971.

The aim of the introduction, and the prologue to each chapter, is to give the reader the historical context for the photographs that follow. In the introduction, the photographs are referred to in the narrative; the aim is to allow the pictures to create their own impression with the minimum of intrusive explanatory captions.

INTRODUCTION

The Habsburg Empire vanished over half a century ago. At noon on November 11th, 1918, the same day that firing ceased on the Western Front and the *war to end all wars* was over, its last Emperor, Charles, signed his decree of abdication. With it ended not only his reign of a mere two years' duration but an empire which had survived nearly four centuries. It began as it ended, through the agency of war. On the battlefield of Mohacs in 1526, the Turks annihilated the Hungarian dynasty which ruled the ancient kingdoms of Bohemia and Hungary. Ferdinand, the Habsburg Archduke of Austria, inherited what was left of their territories. From the outset the Habsburg Empire was an artificial creation. Its three main constituents were: the Czech lands bordering Russia, Poland and the Holy Roman Empire; Hungary which was merely the rump of the great Kingdom of St. Stephen which had once stretched from Vienna to the Balkans; and the heterogeneous Habsburg domain, which became known as Austria. They had nothing in common except their ruler. It was an empire which came eventually to comprise twelve different nationalities, each with its own dialect and local culture. While Austria and Bohemia looked to Western Europe for their model, Hungary, which the Turks were to occupy for centuries, looked always towards the East. Like the Imperial two-headed eagle which the Habsburgs adopted as their emblem, their state had to face both ways at once. Indeed most of the problems of this ill-favoured empire stemmed from the facts of its geography.

When war was declared in 1914, the Habsburg Empire straddled the river Danube from Passau in Germany to the Iron Gates gorge in Roumania. To the north it was bounded by Russia, to the south by Italy and the Adriatic. It covered an area of over a quarter of a million square miles. Its capital, Vienna, was a city of world rank, a polyglot assembly of all the varied nationalities which comprised the empire. Prague was the ancient capital of the Kingdom of Bohemia, closer both in geography and spirit to Paris, Berlin and London than the much newer city of Budapest, the second city of the empire. The provincial centres like Agram, Cracow and Sarajevo had little more than a veneer of western culture, for they remained defiantly nationalist, wanting little from Vienna other than to be left in peace. To these towns and cities must be added, at least for part of the period which this book covers, the great urban centres of Northern Italy—Milan, Venice, Verona, Mantua—which were once part of the empire. Despite these numerous cities, however, the empire was overwhelmingly rural and agricultural, slow-moving and suspicious of change. Its rulers, who generally shared these last two characteristics, saw in the honest peasantry, irrespective of nationality, the fundamental guarantee of the stability of society. To judge the Habsburg Empire of the nineteenth century by the same criteria as we apply to France, Germany or Britain, is entirely wrong. In many respects, by its enormous size, by its leanings towards the East and by its multi-national society, it was much more akin to Russia.

This book deals with the Habsburg Empire in the years following the defeat of Napoleon through to the First World War. During that century it survived recurrent crises: revolution in 1848, disaster in war in 1859 and 1866, economic collapse in 1873, political turmoil during the 1890's. On a more personal level, the dynasty seemed accursed: the brother, son, wife, and heir of the Emperor Francis Joseph all met violent ends. Yet these are the negative aspects. By 1914 the empire was richer, less repressive, and more civilised than ever before in its history. It was not doomed to disaster, condemned to become the new *sick man of Europe*, as many of its enemies claimed. It failed to solve its pressing problems during the nineteenth century but no one really wished to see its demise. As Francis Palacký wrote in the Year of Revolutions, 1848, "If there were no Austria, it would be necessary to create one". Its virtues were negative. It was autocratic yet it protected its subjects from the worse autocracy of Russia or Germany. It was inefficient but less so than its neighbours to the East. Its citizens tolerated its existence but often felt no particular loyalty or affection for it. The Habsburg Empire had lost its mission by the nineteenth century, and was content simply to "muddle through" (*"weiterwursteln"*). This curious state produced a form of society unique in Europe; it has now disappeared utterly. The photographs of this volume are an attempt to reconstruct it.

THE OLD EMPIRE

"Pre-March" is the phrase used to describe the last years between the Congress of Vienna, which re-established the old order in Europe in 1815, and March 1848 when the forces of revolution erupted once again. It was a period of conscious reaction, controlled by Metternich, who like so many servants of the Austrian monarchy was not Austrian at all. One enemy of all that Metternich stood for, Heinrich von Laube, wrote of the great Chancellor:

> Metternich is, for me, the greatest autocrat of recent times. He has, in the teeth of all gales, kept the old threatened Absolutism at the helm of government. He is the current divinity of Absolutism. Homage must be paid to the gods even if they are unloved . . .

It was the age of secret police and surveillance of citizens suspected of liberal tendencies. The policeman (page 41) was feared at all levels of society. It was a rigid, authoritarian society, but quite close to the surface of it lay entirely different forces. The men and women portrayed (pages 29—41), represent the middle classes of the era: an English visitor described these women, apparently so stiff and formal, in critical terms:

> There cannot be a more dissolute city, one where female virtue is less prized, and therefore less frequent. A total want of principle, the love of pleasure, are so widely diffused that wives and daughters . . . do not shrink from increasing the means of their extravagance by forgetting their duty. They sacrifice themselves not so much from inclination as from interest. In Vienna you will find . . . many who throw away their honour for the love of gain.

Their men received little more flattering comment:

> The quantity of licentiousness is commonly smallest among the middle class of a people. It is not so in Vienna, at least among the men. To hear the nonchalance with which a party of respectable merchants speak of their amours, you would think them dissolute bachelors; yet they are husbands and fathers, and . . . it never enters their heads that their conduct has anything improper in it.

Perhaps this is merely the superior priggishness of the English, but the examples of pornographic photography (pages 42—3), which had wide circulation, speak for themselves. The society which grew up in opposition to the archaic autocracy exemplified by Metternich, combining political liberalism, cosy artistic Romanticism, and bourgeois economic values, was known as *Biedermeier*. The word conjures up a homely solidity, thoroughly middle-class, which is remembered best in the furniture of the period. Yet it was these upright citizens who were transformed into revolutionaries.

On the morning of Monday, March 13th, 1848, the old autocracy started to collapse. The spark of revolution had taken root in the Habsburg domains, first in Vienna, then rapidly in Budapest and the cities of north Italy. Prague and Cracow followed suit. Although these outbreaks were part of a movement affecting most of Europe, starting with the overthrow of the Bourbons and the declaration of a republic in France, they had a character of their own throughout the Austrian Empire. Onto the usual constitutional demands for a liberalisation of the regime, were tacked emotive nationalist appeals. The Hungarians and Czechs saw the opportunity to prise a measure of local autonomy from the central authorities in Vienna. Even small minorities demanded proper treatment of their national interests. What convinced the provinces and the territories distant from Vienna that absolutism was on the wane was the news that Metternich had resigned: he personified the unchanging rigidity of the Imperial system. From the moment he fell from power, the orgy of reform began.

It was also a revolution of youth against the archaic and unbending political system for which they felt no sympathy. The Lombard students (page 49) looked and behaved much like their contemporaries in Vienna, Prague and Budapest. They were armed and organised and provided a backbone for the revolution. But like the other revolutionaries, they had little contact with other nationalities or cities in revolt against the Habsburg government. In this lay the great weakness of the many enemies of the state. There was not one revolution but many, far more than the ruling order had means to suppress. What troops there were had been concentrated in Italy where the danger seemed greatest, and under the command of Field Marshal Radetzky order was gradually restored. But soldiers who might serve well enough against Italians could be completely unreliable against their fellow-countrymen. The army was scarcely a reliable prop for the regime, since it too was permeated by revolutionary attitudes. The only means by which the ruling group could regain control was by an absolute and ruthless determination not to compromise. They acted to suppress the centres of revolution piecemeal. Prague surrendered to Prince Alfred Windischgrätz, who used his few troops with brutal effectiveness. Four and a half months later, reinforced and with an even firmer resolve to extirpate the taint of liberalism, he forced the submission of Vienna.

The end of revolution in the west of the Empire meant the virtual isolation of the Hungarians. From the outset their claims had had a very radical tinge. The leader of the revolution in Hungary, Lajos Kossuth (page 50), was a fanatical patriot; in his eyes, the only good that could come from Vienna was an admission of Hungarian independence. In nine months of revolution, the Hungarians had extracted concessions from the Habsburgs which gave them a large measure of liberty, and which they were perfectly prepared to defend by war, if necessary. The issue was forced by a dynastic coup. It had long been planned that the old and rather feeble Emperor Ferdinand should abdicate in favour of his eighteen-year-old nephew Francis Joseph, but neither the Emperor nor the heir to the throne, Francis Joseph's father, seemed eager to renounce their positions. It was not until December 1848 that pressure prevailed and the transfer of power took place. The new Emperor knelt before his uncle, who renounced his thrones; Francis Charles, the next in line of descent, waived his claim, and in this rather covert manner the new reign began. It was to last nearly seventy years.

The Hungarian response to these dynastic manoeuvres was characteristic. They declared that Hungary had not been consulted, that Ferdinand was the only crowned King of Hungary and that they accepted no other. In this situation of crisis, the radicals gained an even firmer control and proclaimed that the "perjured House of Habsburg-Lorraine" was expelled from the throne of Hungary and a Regency established in its place. Only a massive intervention by a Russian army, in the interests of legitimate monarchy, finally caused them to surrender. Seventeen months after the crowds in the streets of Vienna had forced the abdication of Metternich and the collapse of autocracy, the old order was re-established. Although the threat of revolution had disappeared, 1849 marked the beginning of difficulties for the new Emperor. For two decades, the Habsburg Empire produced a string of failures. The great failure after the suppression of the many revolts was to realise that there *were* legitimate grounds for complaint and opposition. The disturbances of March 1848 had had the support of all sections of society, save perhaps the most blue-blooded of the aristocracy. The less die-hard adherents of the revolutionary movements fell away as the demands became more radical, but they had no wish to return to the old system. The settlement imposed by the victorious Francis Joseph and his main adviser Prince Schwarzenberg was politically sterile. Friends and enemies were both treated harshly. The Croats, who had stayed loyal and under their leader Josip Jellačić had invaded Hungary at a crucial point, were shown no favours. The Hungarians were far more savagely repressed than was necessary and the ill-will created was to rebound on the Habsburgs in later years.

The opportunity after 1848, with a new Emperor and a new administration, was to build a more liberal and efficient system than had existed before. When it became clear that this was not going to happen a great sense of disillusion settled on the Habsburg dominions. It produced corruption and inefficiency of almost oriental proportions, for no one dared to criticise the functionaries of the new political order. Mistakes were made on every side. Russia was offended by clumsy Austrian diplomacy during the Crimean War. The economy was mishandled, and large concessions were made to foreign exploiters. Too much of the money earmarked for the army stuck to the hands of the commissariat department and morale, already low, was weakened still further by lack of proper equipment. At the first test, the whole structure crumbled.

The Habsburg Empire was forced into war three times in seven years. In 1859, Napoleon III of France suddenly discovered his rôle as a great liberator of Italy from the yoke of the Austrians. It was a campaign which brought no credit to any of the combatants, but the balance of success lay with the French. The ineptitude of the Austrian commanders was revealed. The strong position won by Radetzky in 1848 was thrown away by timidity. The young Emperor who took command during the campaign in the belief, false as it turned out, that he could win victories where his generals could not, was forced to accept a humiliating peace and the loss of the kingdom of Lombardy. Five years later, in association with Prussia, the empire went to war again, this time with Denmark over the disputed duchies of Schleswig-Holstein. Not unnaturally, they managed to overwhelm the Danes, but in the process acquired an inflated view of their own proficiency. Austrian officers came away from the battlefield with a benign disdain for the Prussians, whom they counted able enough, but dull and uninspired in war. Just how mistaken they were in this judgement was made apparent in the war of 1866. The Prussian master-plan, which lay formulated in the mind of Bismarck, was to force Austria to withdraw from Germany; the only sure way to achieve this was by war. A *casus belli* was found and the shortest and most devastating campaign in the history of the Habsburg Empire began. In a matter of days the true military might of Prussia became apparent. In everything, from their dreaded needle gun to the quality of their boots, they were immeasurably better than their opponents. The Austrians lost battle after battle, often with large casualties. The climax came on July 3rd, 1866. At Königgrätz, on ground chosen by the Austrian commander Benedek, the Prussians won a complete victory. The road to Vienna lay open, and only an impassioned plea by Bismarck, who did not want to humiliate the Austrians more than necessary, dissuaded the Prussian king from a victory march through the streets of the conquered city. Two minor Austrian victories over the Piedmontese, on sea and land, could not disguise the extent of the disaster.

"CASCA IL MONDO" (THE WORLD IS COLLAPSING)
— The Papal Secretary of State, on receiving the news of Königgrätz

With the defeat of Königgrätz and the peace of Prague which soon followed it, the modern history of Austria began. The Prussian terms were not harsh: they demanded neither territory nor crushing financial indemnity as they were to do from the French in 1870. But they insisted that Austria should leave the German Confederation for ever. From that time, the interests of the Habsburg monarchy were turned towards the east. Even if the German element of the population was the most numerous and productive section of the empire, they could no longer claim special treatment as they had done when the possibility of a German Empire under Austrian leadership had existed. The turn towards the east was heightened by the loss of the last Italian province through an unwise agreement made before the war began. The final and most important result of the defeat was that Francis Joseph at last recognised the need for a settlement with the Hungarians. Two wars with a constant threat of rebellion from a sullen Hungary had convinced him that the state could not survive unless normal relations were re-established. He did not relish the prospect, since the Hungarians remained tainted with treason in his eyes. But he sacrificed his personal desires, as he was to do repeatedly, for what he conceived to be the good of the state. A new constitutional arrangement was made, an *Ausgleich* or Compromise reached with Hungary, which created a new state to be known for ever as Austria-Hungary.

It was a state which was unique in history. The two elements, Austria and Hungary, were to remain separate sovereign states, united in the person of their ruler. Thus Francis Joseph ruled as Emperor in Austria and King in Hungary. Each state was to have its own government and political system. Certain functions like war and foreign affairs were carried by institutions acting for both states. There was a joint legislature of sorts which consisted of delegates from the separate Parliaments of Austria and Hungary, who met separately to vote funds to cover the costs of the joint institutions. In effect it meant three bureaucracies instead of one, each jealous of its own prerogatives and reluctant to co-operate with the others. It meant a political system with an infinite potential for delay and inactivity by those so minded, and a perfect paradise for constitutional lawyers. The substance and the minutiae of the constitution remained a constant source of acrimony from the day it was signed until the day it was dissolved. Yet given the extraordinary problems it had to overcome and the irreconcilables which had to be resolved within it, it was not a bad system.

To understand the nature of the Austro-Hungarian monarchy it is first necessary to understand its jargon. The common institutions of the state, including the Emperor himself, were both Imperial and Royal: in German the phrase is *kaiserlich und königlich* — *k. u. k.* for short. That which pertained to Hungary was exclusively Royal, since the Hungarians recognised their ruler only as King of Hungary. Their institutions were *königlich*, abbreviated to *kgl*. The Austrian half on the monarchy, with less attention to punctilio, were content that their institutions should be called Imperial-Royal, *kaiserlich-königlich, k. k.* This profusion of initials indicates the almost Byzantine complexity of the Dual Monarchy, as it came to be known. It is a world caught best by the novelist Robert Musil. He nicknamed Austria-Hungary "Kakania" a world where everything was prefixed by an arrangement of the letter "K":

> Now many remarkable things might be said about that vanished Kakania. For instance, it was *k. k.* (Imperial-Royal) and it was *k. u. k.* (Imperial and Royal); one of the two abbreviations applied to every thing and every person, but esoteric lore was nevertheless required in order to be sure of distinguishing which institutions and persons were to be referred to as *k. k.* and which as *k. u. k.* On paper it called itself the Austro-Hungarian Monarchy; in speaking, however, one referred to it as Austria, that is to say, it was known by a name that it had solemnly renounced as a state . . . By its constitution it was liberal, but its system of government was clerical. Its system of government was clerical, but the general attitude to life was liberal. Before the law all citizens were equal, but not everyone, of course, was a citizen. There was a parliament, which made such vigorous use of its liberty that it was usually kept shut; but there were also emergency powers by means of which it was possible to manage without parliament, and yet each time that everybody was rejoicing in the return of absolutism the Crown ordered that there must be parliamentary rule again.

15

It is not surprising that this state, where all power and initiative suffered modification by a thousand qualifications and impediments, should have been neither progressive nor very efficient. It was an attempt at a working multi-national state, severely flawed from the outset; it survived, however, for over half a century. The society which it created has no parallel, and even today reminders of it survive in the nationalities which once comprised the Dual Monarchy.

THE IMAGE OF THE EMPIRE

Hidden in documents and history books are clues to the nature of life under the Austro-Hungarian monarchy. Amid the mass of statistics which the myriad officials regularly produced lie the bare facts of life: the number of acres owned by the great family of Esterházy, the daily rate of pay of a factory worker in Steyr, the incidence of bad feet on the desolate army posts of Galicia. The photographs in this book provide a different kind of record. The camera had begun as an expensive toy but by the First World War photography was a popular craze. It embraced everything and everyone; emperors sat in their state robes in front of the camera, as did shop girls and their beaux on a Sunday outing. Technical progress had soon made it possible for almost anyone to be his own photographer. It was a society devoted to the family snapshot and the photograph album; but except in a few cases, they were not thought of as historic documents. Their value is oblique, for today we have no interest in the individual personalities of the forgotten society ladies or anonymous working men who stare out from these pages. But they capture in a single image facets of that past world which no historian or statistician would have thought worth recording. The aristocratic lady and the nanny (page 135), and the Hungarian peasants at market (page 198—99), Jews in their Polish ghetto (page 234—35) or the two dreary officers on manoeuvres (page 305), are eloquent testimonials to the nature of Austrian society. Their worth lies in the extra detail that no one actually intended to record: the clothes, the passers-by, the shop signs, all the trivia of daily life. Through them we can build up a rounded picture of the whole society, as it existed until 1918.

Of all the classes which made up the monarchy, the least affected by the dramatic changes of the nineteenth century was the aristocracy. The backbone of the noble families were the great patrician dynasties. Some, like the Liechtensteins and Khevenhüllers, had been a power in Austria long before the rise of the Habsburgs. The Windischgrätz intermarried with the royal houses of Europe and the great nobles of Hungary, like the Esterházy (page 136), lived like princes. The huge palace of Esterháza rivalled Versailles. The strength of the nobility lay in their estates, which were both vast and rich, although not many could equal the Schwarzenbergs (page 141) who owned over 300,000 acres of Bohemia or the Esterházys with over 700,000 acres in Hungary. Their style of life had changed little for generations in its ordered regular pattern, with shooting in season and a regular stay in Vienna and the appropriate spa; hunting *à l'anglaise* (pages 145, 260—61) had its devotees, and all Society frequented the race course, either the great festive occasions of Prague, Vienna or Budapest (pages 131—33, 188) or in some provincial town. In many ways, the life they led was close to that of the Anglo-Irish Ascendency. Below the greatest families, who ruled virtual principalities, were the lesser nobility with more moderate lands and finally the poor gentry, who were more actively concerned with the exploitation of their lands. The nobility of the Austro-Hungarian monarchy never lost its close connection with its estates and even the mightiest magnates paid regular attention to tiny details of estate management; the only exceptions were the Polish aristocrats of Galicia, who abandoned their barren estates and surly peasantry to new proprietors, frequently Jewish. The general picture of the nobility in the empire is of an excessively privileged but not entirely useless group. They benefited most from the antique nature of Austrian society; as one contemporary writer sourly commented: "That state today is still the tool of the noble."

If the aristocracy lent a certain hauteur to the social life of the Dual Monarchy, it was the middle classes which created its real character. They had grown enormously in numbers since the 1840's, combining the professional classes—the doctors, lawyers and university teachers who had made the revolution of 1848—with the new rich, the men of commerce and industry. Although the empire remained predominantly rural, the number of towns had increased dramatically in the space of fifty years; these new or vastly expanded towns were the cradle of a strong middle class, and were concentrated very heavily in the western half of the monarchy. Places like Linz (page 243), Salzburg (page 245) and Graz (page 241) flourished with the growth of trade, and the small spa towns like Karlsbad (pages 248—50), Marienbad and Bad Ischl became thriving resorts. Everywhere the middle classes came to exercise a dominant role; the army, which in other countries had a strongly aristocratic bias, was in Austria-Hungary the province of the bourgeoisie, and the vast bureaucracy was middle-class almost to a man, as was the press, the stock-market and the professions. In Vienna, their comfortable "*gemütlich*" world found its natural home, with a colourful medley of the various nationalities of the empire providing a background for a tolerant and flexible code of behaviour. It was a very feminine society, dedicated to gossip and the pursuit of trivia. The Viennese woman (pages 89, 92, 96) had not, in the words of one contemporary writer:

> the refined grace, the conversational gifts, the lightness of touch of the *Parisienne*, but she has nothing in common with the meticulous and diligent ingenuity of the Prussian

"Hausfrau", that lover of order, impervious to good taste; she knows how to dress well, she is devoted to the theatre and sport, and she is exceptionally gifted in the art of pleasing men, foreigners even more than natives.

But this was the apogee of the middle-class ideal. Much more typical were the wives of local officials in dismal provincial towns, bored with the society of their few neighbours (page 273). For the German-speaking middle-class much of the empire was as foreign as Africa or India. Their aspirations were not those of the high aristocracy for they had little interest in the world beyond the city; from their ranks was created a new aristocracy of service. Army officers with sufficient years of duty or successful industrialists were rewarded with a title; but they remained entirely bourgeois, both in their way of life and their outlook. They were the true creators of a specifically Austro-Hungarian culture.

Nothing could provide a stronger contrast with their comfortable, stable lives than the condition of the working class. Wages were low and living costs high, and particularly in Vienna, accommodation was almost impossible to find. The workers' flats (pages 102—3) were little more than

> great barracks, five storeys high, with thousands of windows... The streets are empty; only here and there herds of dirty children play in the putrid water of the street. Enter any door and you will discover the same scene: a little dark staircase, with black greasy walls ... strange corridors each with an infinity of numbered doors, each of which is the entrance to a workman's dwelling. It is almost always a single room; sometimes two hundred families live in one barracks. (1913)

Although these dreadful conditions were equalled in London, Paris or Berlin, they were infinitely more acute in the Habsburg Empire. For although conditions were bad in the cities they seemed a better alternative to an endless life of rural servitude (page 244). The farm workers drifted to the cities or emigrated overseas; by the First World War, the United States in particular had received large numbers of immigrants glad to be free from the despair they had known under the Dual Monarchy. One manifestation of this sense of hopelessness was the high rate of suicide among the working classes. Although the lot of all sections of the working class was unenviable, none was worse than that of women. At every turn they faced exploitation: if they went to work in a factory (page 106), their wages were much lower than those of men, with no security of employment. If they took the easier option and entered domestic service, they became household drudges. The work of a nursery maid (page 135) was paradise compared with that of the housemaid or under-cook. There were affluent workers, skilled mechanics and technicians, who had benefited from the growth of industry, but they were fewer in number than in other industrialised European countries. The bulk of Austrian society worked for the benefit of the few, the aristocracy and the middle class; it was a highly unstable situation. Yet there was no catalyst which could transform discontent into revolution.

The running sore of the empire was not class division but the problem of nationalism. In the fifty years of its existence, there was not one in which Austria-Hungary was not troubled by rivalry between two or more races. There were long-standing disputes, like that between Czechs and Germans in Bohemia, or occasional explosions, as between Croats and Italians in the region of Trieste: racial tensions could never be overlooked. There were those who made political capital out of this situation, like the wily Count Taaffe, who was Francis Joseph's most successful minister. His programme and stated objective was to keep the races in "a state of well-modulated discontent", allowing him to play one faction off against another. The effect of racial conflict was political stagnation since none of the long-standing problems facing the empire could be tackled without the risk of turmoil. At the base of most difficulties lay the Compromise of 1867 and the peculiarly privileged position it gave to the Hungarians: Czechs, Slavs from the South and Ruthenes demanded an equal amount of liberty. But every attempt to redress the balance met with an absolute veto by Hungary, who added point to their refusal by denying the government its tax-revenue. It was an impasse; innumerable panaceas were produced designed to create a stable system, but not one of them was remotely practicable in political terms. To cap this already explosive situation there existed another racial problem, that of the Jews. There were over two million of them within the confines of the monarchy, ranging from the pathetic inhabitants of the ghetto (pages 187, 234—35), or rural Galicia (page 266), to the princely Jewish dynasties of banking and commerce such as the Rothschilds. Budapest was so dominated by Jewish professional men that it was nicknamed "Jewdapest". Anti-semitism was rife at all levels of Austro-Hungarian society, and was often indeed the only common factor between the warring nationalities. Austria-Hungary produced Adolf Hitler, and many others with an equally vicious hatred of Jewish success, but anti-semitism was only one manifestation of the violent racial undercurrents in the Dual Monarchy.

The alpha and omega of the empire, the informing spirit behind every decision, was the Emperor himself. His character was complex and the very length of his reign, almost seventy years, makes it hard to connect the stately, bewhiskered old gentleman (pages 153, 295) with the dashing young man of eighteen who came to the throne in 1848. Very few characteristics stayed with him throughout his long life, but of these, three were vital. His Catholic religion was genuinely and deeply felt, and in the many moments of crisis which came his way he found support in the ceremonies of the Church. In early years his religious fervour, the product of a clerical education, left too much influence with his confessor and the dignitaries of the Church; but he soon learned to temper piety with political caution. His capacity for work

19

was prodigious. He rose at 4.0 a.m. and worked till breakfast; lunch was at twelve, and dinner at five. State papers, from the great state treaties down to the daily routine of military cadets, went to him, were carefully annotated and passed for action. His routine was inflexible: Sir Frederick Ponsonby records how when the British King, Edward VII, visited Vienna:

> It was difficult at first to bring the two monarchs together. The Emperor got up at 4.0 a.m. . . . The King on the other hand didn't have his coffee till 10.0 a.m., and although he had of course to conform to the Emperor's times for meals, he was quite unable to go to bed at 7.30 p.m. when the Emperor retired.

But despite his dedication, he could never hope to keep pace with the flood of paperwork needing his attention. Like his ancestor Philip II of Spain, whom he resembled in several respects, he simply provided a further hindrance to effective government. But probably the most significant clue to his character lies in his view of himself. From his earliest years he thought of himself as a simple soldier. He revelled in the ceremony and regimentation of military life; he was rarely seen out of uniform. Every year he attended manoeuvres, a stiff slim figure on horseback even in his sixties (page 301). *His* army was the main focus of his attention, the only subject which could ever rouse him to passion or interest. He sought to create in the state the same orderly military virtues that he valued in his officers and men.

He became by the end of the nineteenth century a venerable curiosity. He outlived Queen Victoria by fifteen years; he was, as he proudly told Theodore Roosevelt, "the last European monarch of the old school". By the last years of his life, he was raised above the enmities of nationality or politics and was venerated even by the sworn foes of his empire. One Slav who intended to assassinate the Emperor found himself unable to pull the trigger as the old man passed by at point-blank range in front of him. Yet he was never a warm or human character; although he was a man of highly developed passions, he was always aware of his Imperial position, and perhaps this inhibited him in his relationships even with those closest to him. The storms of his marriage to Elizabeth seem to have been due much more to her instability than to his failings, for he was a model of devoted affection. His relationship with his son Rudolph was unhappy, and only with his grandchildren did he seem really at ease. He became the personification of his people.and his empire: old-fashioned, honourable, and an anachronism in a twentieth century world. This present book is a scrapbook of varied impressions of his long life and reign.

ANDREW WHEATCROFT

In 1855 Artaria, the Viennese publishing house famous for its engravings and maps, brought out this *Karte der Oesterreichischen Monarchie* (Map of the Austrian Monarchy) · The description "Austria-Hungary" would have been appropriate only after the so-called "Compromise" of 1867 which divided the Austrian Empire into Austrian and Hungarian halves · The territories of Trieste, Gorizia, Gradiska, Istria, Carinthia and Krain are here summarily comprised under the title *Illyrien* (Illyria), adopted from the kingdom of that name founded by Napoleon · The *Militärgrenze* (military frontier), created in the first half of the eighteenth century against the Turks and not dissolved until 1881, is still divided into its *croatisch-slavonisch* (Croatian-Slavonian) and *banatisch-serbisch* (Banat-Serb) portions. The *Lombardisch-Venetianisches Königreich* (Lombard-Venetian kingdom), whose components were to be lost in 1859 and 1866 respectively, is clearly demarcated · Bosnia and Hercegovina, on the other hand, still belong to the *Türkisches Reich* (Turkish empire), coming under the Austrian crown only in 1878 by way of the occupation sanctioned at the Congress of Berlin

KRONLÄNDER der OESTERREICH. MONARCHIE

I	a	Oesterreich unter der Enns	
	b	Oesterreich ob der Enns	
	c	Salzburg	
II		Tirol	
III		Steyermark	
IV	A	Triest / Görz. Gradisca u. Istrien	Illyrien
	B	Kärnthen	
	C	Krain	
V		Dalmatien	
VI		Lombard. Venetianisches Königr.	
VII		Böhmen	
VIII	a	Mähren	
	b	Schlesien	
IX	a	Galizien und Lodomerien etc. nebst	
		Krakau	
	b	Bukowina	
X		König. Ungarn	
XI		Croatien und Slavonien	
XII		Serb. Woiwodschaft und Banat	
XIII		Siebenbürgen	
1		Croatisch-Slavonische	Militär-Grenze
2		Banatisch-Serbische	

ZEICHEN-ERKLÄRUNG

⦿ HAUPT UND RESIDENZ STÆDTE

● Hauptstädte

⦁ Städte überhaupt

· Flecken und Dörfer

⊛ Feste Plätze

— Eisenbahnen

Maassstäbe

Deutsche Meilen 15 = 1°

Italienische Meilen 60 = 1°

AUTHOR'S PREFACE

Many years ago I chanced on a small book which meanwhile has taken its place in my library in a number of editions—*Wurstelprater*, published 1908 in Vienna and written with acute observation and critical detachment by Felix Salten, author of *Bambi*, on the subject of the amusement park, world-famous during its heyday in pre-First World War Vienna. The small photographs, taken by Dr. Emil Mayer and facing each page, fascinated me. I was already on the staff of *Magnum*, the periodical where a public that barely found time any more for reading, was brought into contact with the problems of our contemporary world by visual means. These early specimens of really live photography were a revelation to me. I pored over them, again and again, magnifying glass in hand: here the old Dual Monarchy, the multinational state of Slavs, Magyars, Italians, Germans, sprang to life. In Vienna all these races had fused. To look at these pictures was to understand the character of the Viennese and their origins.

For years I searched for the originals of the photos until a series of copies and then slides fell by accident into my hands. From these enlargements could be made. As a by-product, so to speak, of my search I also lit on other historic photos. The outcome was a book with pictures of Vienna as it had once been, a publication due in the last analysis to the promptings of artist friends. For my part, thanks to Dr. Mayer's fascinating photographs, I continued to be haunted by the notion of a work which would take in the whole of the Monarchy.

Was it feasible, I wondered, to track down such photographic documentation of the enormous territory formerly belonging to the multinational state (now situated preponderantly inside the Soviet-dominated bloc) as would render manifest something of the world familiar to us through the novels of Joseph Roth and Robert Musil, through Kafka, Johannes Urzidil, Doderer and Alexander Lernet-Holenia, through the stories of our parents and the older generation, as well as through the tales of Roda-Roda and Eichthal, Lehár operettas and Hollywood films? What had it really been like? Drawings and paintings present visual images, but the danger of idealization is inherent. Photography is, to me, the tough form of documentation. For all that it may distort and exaggerate, it remains realistic, perhaps precisely because of the lens' all-inclusiveness which does not excise apparent irrelevancies and thus often effects telling disclosures. In Europe photography's documentary quality was in the past never so fully appreciated as in America. Consequently many pictures were thrown away or destroyed because (this happens even now) they were "only photos". Few photographs were made of everyday life, even fewer of that featuring the lower classes, and technical reasons were not the sole explanation. Only towards the end of the nineteenth century did snapshots become easier to take, but in this field too American photographers were ahead of Europeans in a critical approach to social themes. As early as the American Civil War Brady's teams of cameramen visited all the scenes of conflict. The Library of Congress at Washington possesses more than ten thousand prints shot by them, whereas we have hardly a single picture of the battle of Königgrätz in 1866. What, under such auspices and with two World Wars between, could be expected?

For me there began a fresh quest lasting for years. Innumerable trips through the lands and cities of the former Empire, to country mansions, to smaller and larger local museums, and calls on people in private life to whom I had been given introductions, members of the nobility in Croatia and Hungary, Bohemia and Austria. Failures abounded. In Czernowitz, today across the Russian border, nothing was left. In Hungarian towns and villages, especially in Budapest, much had been destroyed by fighting. I could dig out some treasures, but a lot may continue to rest undiscovered in private ownership. On the whole, though, my hunt was successful.

The old photographers must forgive the liberties I have taken with their work. For me their pictures are a vicarious reality. I go through them (as my friend Alfred Schmeller puts it) with *Magnum* eyes: I see there what *I* would have seen at the time. A great deal of what I had in mind as part of my history was not available and stayed wishful thinking. More often than I wanted, rather less vivid photographs had to be included for history's sake.

Now we have the upshot—notwithstanding that certain aspects are missing, a rounded picture of the vanished world of yesterday.

FRANZ HUBMANN

PRE-MARCH

The years between the tranquil elegance of the Congress of Vienna and March 1848, when the streets of Vienna resounded with the cries of revolution, have a strange character. The Austrians, once noted for their expansive gaiety, turned in upon themselves and settled into domesticity. But in Metternich's police state they could do little else. It was an interlude between the old settled world of the Eighteenth Century and the turbulent changes of the Nineteenth.

The point usually overlooked is that it was precisely during this time that technology began to get into its stride and the new industrial age was born.

Early in the nineteenth century, it was often the French, Swiss and English innovators who set up textile, sugar and paper factories, iron foundries and similar undertakings in the Habsburg lands. In 1816 the first steam-driven machine was installed; in 1829 the Danube Steamship Company was founded; in 1832 the Linz—Budweis horse-drawn railway began operations, and in 1838 the first train travelled the twenty miles from Vienna to Wagram.

A year later photography arrived from France. The first contract signed by its inventors, Nièpce and Daguerre, proclaimed its purpose: "To portray nature without the aid of an artist". During the initial dozen years photographs were single specimens on silver plates which, given a certain exposure, effected a picture with very delicately differentiated shadings. Then, in 1851, Archer, an Englishman, contrived a process whereby prints could be made from layered glass-plates. To that invention we owe our reproductions, the image of Austrians during an epoch usually familiar to us only by way of paintings and drawings.

Elderly Biedermeier gentleman · Daguerreotype in gold-coloured paper
frame · About 1844 · Photographer unknown

33

Eduard Witting, a Viennese silk
ribbon manufacturer · Daguerreotype
miniature · 1846 · Photographer
unknown

Pauline Gassenbauer, Edle von Heid
Daguerreotype miniature · 1846
Photographer unknown

Officer in dark tunic · Daguerreotype
About 1843 · Photographer unknown

37   Biedermeier villa on the outskirts of Vienna · Daguerreotype · About 1842—1845 · Photographer unknown

Portrait of an elderly lady in front of a tapestry · Photograph by Anton C. Martin, Assistant Lecturer at the University of Technology, Vienna, taken during a trip to Silesia, 1840—1841 · Martin was Austria's first amateur photographer and the author of a manual on photography

Page 38: A senior Treasury official, Schultz von Strasnitzki · Daguerreotype · 1845 Photographer unknown

Page 39: Biedermeier lady wearing a turban · Stereo Daguerreotype · About 1847 · Photographer unknown

Page 41: Karl Lazarus (Lazzer), a police official of the Metternich Era · Daguerreotype · 1845 Photographer unknown

Biedermeier pornography · Photographs of this
type sold in large quantities · About 1847
Photographer unknown

Right: Sketch of a nude in the manner of Ingres
Daguerreotype · About 1848 · Photographer
unknown

Top: The Cathedral of Gran (Esztergom) under construction · Daguerreotype · About 1846 · Photographer
unknown. St Stephen, Hungary's most famous king, was crowned at Gran, at that time capital of Hungary
At the cathedral's consecration in 1856 Franz Liszt conducted the mass which he had composed for the occasion
Right: Horse and carriage, with "the Master and Mistress" and two footmen, on a country estate · One
of the rare specimens of open-air photography of a moving object · Daguerreotype · 1841 · Photographer
unknown

Karlsbad
Daguerreotype · 1840 · Photographer unknown
Goethe, from 1785 onward, visited Karlsbad twelve times
in all · The view here may well be as he last saw it

REVOLUTIONS
VICTORIES
DEFEATS

The century of comparative peace between the close of the Napoleonic Wars and the outbreak of World War I suffered one interruption—the turbulent period between 1848 and 1866. During those years the Habsburg Empire was for the first time shaken to its very foundations.

What differentiated the 1848 revolution from happenings in other countries was its character—especially in Hungary and Italy—of being not simply a social but also a national event. In Budapest the poet Petöfi and the politician Kossuth issued a call to arms against Habsburg hegemony, in northern Italy Field Marshal Radetzky, Governor of Lombardy and Venetia, after severe fighting had to evacuate Milan and Lombardy and withdraw to the safety of the so-called Quadrilateral, the defensive area formed by the fortresses of Peschiera—Verona—Legnago—Mantua, and from Vienna the Imperial Court had to flee first to Innsbruck and later to Olmütz.

Then in Prague Field Marshal Windischgrätz, Governor of Bohemia, trampled the revolt underfoot; against Vienna he made common cause with Jellačić, Governor of Croatia; in the case of Hungary, though, it was necessary to call in help from the Tsar. Radetzky gained an annihilating victory against the Piedmontese at Custozza, but he died a few years later. In 1859 Lombardy had finally to be relinquished after the defeat at Solferino where Francis Joseph, twenty-eight years old, had been in personal command of the army against Napoleon III. As late as 1864 Austria was fighting as Prussia's ally against Denmark. While troops advanced towards Jutland, Tegetthoff enjoyed a triumph in the naval skirmish off Heligoland, the last between wooden men-of-war. But in 1866 the Austrians lost the leadership of Germany to Prussia at Königgrätz and Venetia, despite Tegetthoff's victory at Lissa, also had to be evacuated. A year later the Emperor saw himself forced to make far reaching concessions to Hungary in the so-called "Compromise".

The Austro-Hungarian Monarchy was born.

Historians date this daguerreotype as probably having been taken in 1848, the Year of
Revolutions · That would make it a rare photographic record · Its subject seems to be a group
of Lombard students, with their teacher, during the Italian uprising · It is apparently
a victory celebration and the disfigured uniform caps are presumably booty taken from
the Austrians · Photographer unknown

Officers of the Milan garrison, about 1860 · At that time dragoons and cuirassiers still wore shining breastplates · Photographer unknown
Right: A photograph taken on May 11, 1856, of Field Marshal Johann Joseph Wenzel, Count Radetzky von Radetz, at the age of ninety · He, Prince Windischgrätz, and the Croat Governor Jellačić were the three pillars of the Habsburg dynasty during the chaotic days of 1848—9. He began his military career during the eighteenth century, fought against Napoleon, and provided the one great triumph of Austrian arms in 1848, with a victory over the Piedmontese at Custozza
Photo: Kaiser, Verona

Lajos Kossuth, one of the leaders of the Hungarian uprising of 1848 and a fiery revolutionary · Forced into exile after the failure of the revolution, he remained a threat to the Habsburg monarchy until his death in 1894
His son carried on the family tradition of opposition · Photographer unknown

50

51

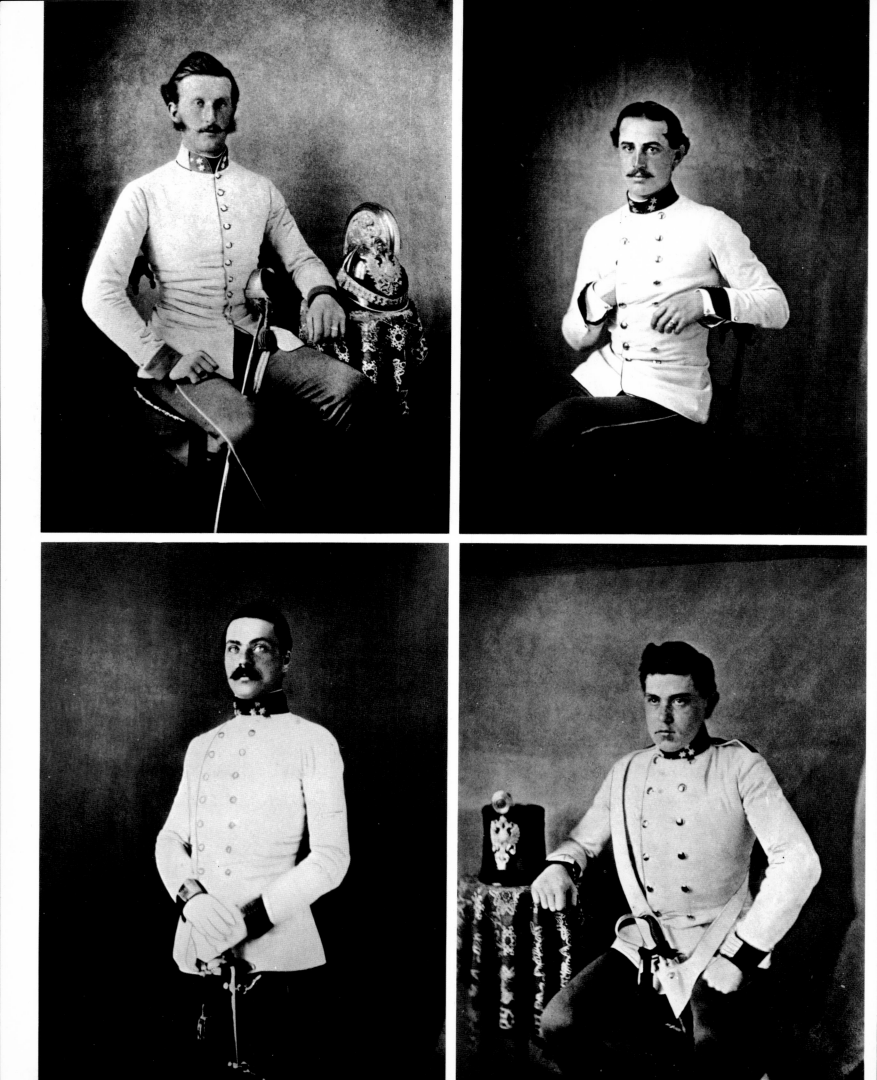

Left: A white tunic was the characteristic uniform of
Austrian officers before 1866 · After that fateful year
it disappeared as offering too easy a target
Photographer unknown

Hermannstadt (Sibiu) in Transylvania
A view of the main square, 1856 · Photographer unknown

Verona, Fort John · About 1860 · Photo: M. Lotze, Verona

Verona, Fort Clam
About 1860
Photo: M. Lotze, Verona

Verona, fortress entrance
About 1860
Photo: M. Lotze, Verona

Venice, fortifications · The port battery Alberone
About 1860 · Photographer unknown

Training with the 15 cm. mounted gun,
Mark M. 1861 · Photographer unknown

Peschiera, Fort Monte Croce · 1861
Photo: M. Lotze, Verona

Right: Peschiera, bridge over the Mincio · 1861
Photo: M. Lotze, Verona
Page 58/59: Venice, Austrian soldiers inside the
fortifications · In the foreground, coastal battery
gun, Mark M. 1859 · In the background, covered
battery · About 1860 · Photographer unknown

Lieutenant Nosinić, Imperial Mexican Army · Maximilian, brother of the
Emperor Francis Joseph, was made Emperor of Mexico with French
support · When the venture failed, Maximilian was abandoned by his allies,
captured by his enemies and shot by a firing squad on June 19, 1867 · His
army was composed of volunteers, like Lieutenant Nosinić dressed in
outlandish uniforms. Their excessively baggy trousers aroused the ridicule
of street urchins · Photographer unknown

H. M. S. *Marlborough*, the flagship of Admiral Fremantle, on a visit to Pola in 1863 · Photographer unknown

The cemetery at Melegnano, near Milan, after its defence by the 16th Company of Infantry Regiment No. 11, on June 8, 1859 · The withdrawal engagement was one of those fought between the battles of Magenta and Solferino · The photo was taken by an unidentified French photographer

Right: "The Imperial Royal Arad Hussars Volunteers Division, No. 2 Squadron · Seated: Lieut. Akos Baron Bruckenthal, Senior Captain Edmund Count Wickenburg, Lieut. Peter von Vuja · Standing: 2/Lieut. Paul von Tóth, Junior Captain Anton Stefezius." The Volunteers were on their way to the Italian theatre of operations · Photo: F. Segl, Salzburg 1859

K.k. Arader Freiwill. Husaren Division.
II Escadron
F. Seql, Photograph in Salzburg No 170.

Right: Venice, concert by the band of the Austrian garrison on St Mark's Square · About 1861 · Amateur photo
Below: Venice, Austrian lagoon flotilla in front of the Church of San Giorgio · In the centre, the screw-driven gunboat *Ausluger,* in the righthand background, the paddle-steamer *Alnoch* · Also five paddle-gunboats of the Types I to VI · About 1864 · Photographer unknown

Page 66: Rear Admiral Wilhelm von Tegetthoff on his flagship *Schwarzenberg* after the naval action off Heligoland on May 9, 1864 · Photo: C. Jounod, Prussian Court Photographer
Page 67: Tegetthoff, with his crew, on board the screw-driven *Schwarzenberg* on June 6, 1864, at Cuxhaven Photographer unknown

In 1864, the Austrians and Prussians co-operated in the invasion
of Schleswig-Holstein, two duchies claimed from
Denmark · A joint force of occupation was established, but the two
countries soon squabbled · The war of 1866
(and Austria's expulsion from Germany) was the result

Centre: Austrian guard at Gottorp castle near Schleswig · 1864
Photographer unknown
Foot: Church parade for Austrian soldiers at Vejle, Jutland
1864 · Photo: Kaysen, Vejle

Austrian Northern Army staff, Königgrätz · 1866 · Photographer unknown · Much of the
responsibility for the failures of the war of 1866 lay with these staff officers
The commander, Benedek, was a loyal and efficient soldier, but with little intellectual training
He relied overmuch on his lazy and inefficient staff

Above: Austrian unit preparing to leave Cracow for Bohemia · 1866 · From left to right, Sgt. August Schiefner, Sgt. Valentin Grüner (wounded at Königgrätz, died in Prussian captivity), Sgt. Anton Fritsch, Sgt. Anton Jaschke, died on the battlefield of Gitschin
Photographer unknown

Left: The naval harbour of Pola, with the *Schwarzenberg*, after the Battle of Lissa · 1866
Photo: Czihak, Vienna

Above: Königgrätz · 1866
Photographer unknown
Below: Lissa, Monument
to the dead of 1866
Photo: Beer, Klagenfurt

Page 72: The screw-driven
corvette *Erzherzog Friedrich*
off Dalmatia · 1868 · The
vessel, which had two years
earlier taken part in the
battle of Lissa, was on
its way to a two years cruise
in Far Eastern waters
Photo: W. Burger, Vienna

VIENNA

When photography was invented, the "Capital and Residence, Vienna" was still enclosed by walls and bastions. Not until 1857 did Francis Joseph, beginning with the well-known words "It is My Pleasure...", issue the order for them to be razed and so prepare the way for the unification of the suburbs with the Inner City. The population then totalled 569,177 inhabitants.

The transmutation into a metropolis and city of international stature was under way. Work started on the Ring, an avenue of a splendour appropriate to the capital of this Empire. In the suburbs the tenement-houses sprouted out of the ground and provided quarters for the second- and third-born peasant sons, artisans and workers who descended on the centre of the Monarchy from all its outlying parts. A patchwork of tribes brightened the streets— Bohemian cooks and maidservants, Italian musicians, Czech nannies, Croat peasant women, Galician Jews, Iglauer wet-nurses, Slovak pedlars, Bosnian infantry and other colourfully accoutred military figures. For them Vienna was the "Golden City" and a visit to the Prater their sole form of Sunday recreation. They swayed to the sound of Strauss waltzes and Lehár's *Merry Widow* set out on its global conquest as twilight enveloped the Empire's glory.

In 1910 the population of Vienna topped the two million mark. A quarter was Bohemian by origin. Not even Prague had that number of Czechs.

Above: The Old Burgtheater, Michaelerplatz · About 1870
It was in use from 1741 to 1888 · Photographer unknown
Right: The Heidenschuss · About 1872 · Photo: W. Burger, Vienna
Page 75: View from the Naschmarkt, across the Elisabeth Bridge, towards St Stephen's
Cathedral · 1872 · The eight statues of historic figures which at that date embellished the
bridge now stand on the Rathausplatz · Photo: W. Burger, Vienna

Right: Horse-drawn streetcar on the Praterstrasse · About 1872 · Photo: W. Burger, Vienna
Below: Market on Am Hof · About 1870 · The square was the scene of many historic events
In 1782 Pope Pius VI blessed the populace from the balcony of the Nine Angel Choirs Church
In 1806 Francis II proclaimed here the dissolution of the Holy Roman Empire · On
March 14, 1848, the attack on the arsenal set off the revolution during the course of which
War Minister Count Latour was beaten to death here and strung up on a lamp-post
Photo: W. Burger, Vienna

Augarten Bridge · About 1870 · Photo: W. Burger, Vienna

Eine Escadron des Uhlanen-Regimentes Fürst zu Schwarzenberg Nr. 2.

Ein k. k. Hofeinspanier
Ein k. k. Hoffourier   } zu Pferde.
Ein k. k. Kammerfourier

Die k. k. Kämmerer und geheimen Räthe zu Pferde. und zwar paarweise:

Die k. k. Kämmerer:

Oberlt. Wilhelm Freiherr v. Hauer
Lieut. Conrad Ritter v. Goldegg
Graf Conrad Weißenwolf
Lieut. Graf Christian Sizzo-Noris
Lieut. Graf Felix Pachta
Oberlt. Baron d'Ablaing
Oberlt. Graf Crenneville
Oberlt. Graf Anton Goëß
Rudolf Freiherr von Stillfried
Graf Philipp Sternberg
Rittmeister Graf Alphons Montecuccoli
Major Graf Wolkenstein
Oberlt. Freiherr von Wittenbach
Graf Georg Larisch-Moennich
Oberlt. Heinrich Freiherr von Trauttenberg
Graf Zdenko Kinsky
Oberlt. Eduard Freiherr von Wucherer
Rittmeister Graf Harnoncourt
Rittmeister Wilhelm Freiherr von Kotz
Major von Bolla
Rittmeister Eduard Freiherr von Wiedersperg
Lieut. Graf Franz Clam-Gallas
Graf Band. Mniszech
Graf Heinrich Larisch-Moennich
Oberlt. Graf Georg Esterházy
Oberlt. Graf Franz Thun
Oberlt. Graf Lad. Cavriani
Rittmeister Graf Carl Chorinsky
Flügel-Adjutant Major Graf Rosenberg
Rittmeister Freiherr von Restorff
Rittmeister Graf Hugo Kálnoky
Rittmeister Graf Hans Nostitz
Rittmeister Freiherr von Dlauhowesky
Heinrich Graf Dubsky
Rittmeister Graf Franz Kinsky
Rittmeister Graf Choloniewski
Heinrich Freiherr von Gudenus
Rittmeister Graf Gabor Festetics
Rittmeister Graf Günther Stolberg
Major Graf Alois Paar
Leopold Freiherr von Ludwigstorff
Rittmeister Graf Leopold Thurn
Rittmeister Graf Spaur
Generalmajor, Graf Eduard Paar
Major Graf Heinrich Lamberg
Oberst Graf Wenzel Festetics
Oberstlt. Emerich Freiherr von Mecséry
Rittmeister Graf Fried. Carl Kinsky
Oberst Freiherr von Bechtolsheim
Graf Arthur Henckel
Rittmeister Graf Ladislaus Thun
Graf Josef Vincenz Waldstein
Oberstlt. Graf Carl Coreth

Major Graf Franz Sickingen
Oberstlt. Graf Anton Schönfeld
Graf Sigismund Berchtold
Rittmeister Graf Eduard Stadion
Rittmeister Graf Alfred Harrach
Rittmeister Graf Felix Vetter
Graf Johann Harrach
FML. Graf Joseph Waldstein
Generalmajor Graf Török
Graf Nako
Graf Erwin Schönborn
Oberlt. Prinz Alain Rohan
Major Prinz Louis Esterhazy
Oberst Prinz Rudolph Liechtenstein
Fürst Starhemberg

J. J. E. E. die k. k. wirkl. geheimen Räthe:

Generalmajor Obersthofmeister Graf Palffy
Major Graf Franz Meran
FML. Freiherr von Salis
Victor Graf Dubsky
FML. Freiherr von Jovanovics
FML. Freiherr von Blasits
Reichs-Kriegs-Minister FML. Graf Bylandt
Graf Mannsfeld
FZM. Freiherr von Ziemiecki
FZM. Freiherr von Packeny
General-Adjutant FML. Freiherr von Beck
Oberstküchenmeister Graf Kinsky
FML. von Latour
Oberstjägermeister Graf Traun
S. D. Fürst Adolph Joseph Schwarzenberg
S. D. Fürst Emil Fürstenberg

Die k. k. geheimen Räthe und Kämmerer im eigenen zweispännigen Galawagen mit ihrer an und neben dem Wagen gehenden Dienerschaft und zwar:

In den Galawägen.

Die k. k. Kämmerer:

Markgraf Alexander Pallavicini
Graf Joseph Baworowski
S. D. Fürst Dietrichstein
S. D. Fürst Franz Joseph Auersperg
S. D. Fürst Khevenhüller

J. J. E. E. die k. k. wirkl. geheimen Räthe:

Graf Guido Karácsony
Graf Wilhelm Siemienski
Graf Julius Andrassy
Graf Ferdinand Trauttmansdorff
Graf Ernst Waldstein
General der Cavallerie Graf Clam-Gallas
S. Erl. Graf Franz Harrach
Se. fürstl. Gnaden Fürst Clary
Fürst Kinsky
S. E. Minister des kaiserlichen Hauses Freiherr von Haymerle
S. D. Fürst Metternich
S. D. Fürst Schönberg
S. D. Fürst Colloredo-Mannsfeld

S. D. Fürst Johann Adolph Schwarzenberg
S. D. Fürst Carlos Auersperg
S. E. der k. k. Obersthofmarschall Graf Larisch-Moennich
S. Em. der Cardinal Fürsterzbischof Landgraf Fürstenberg.

Sechs k. k. Hoftrompeter zu Pferde.

Die Hoflivre und Dienerschaft paarweise.

Zwei k. k. Hoffouriere zu Fuß.

Ein sechsspänniger viersitziger Hofwagen mit den vier k. k. Kämmerern vom Dienste: Die Herren:

Otto Graf Chotek
Carl Graf Pötting und Persing
Rudolph Graf Khevenhüller-Metsch
Arthur Henricourt, Graf von Grünne.

An jedem Schlage ihres Wagens geht ein k. k. Leiblakai

Ein sechsspänniger zweisitziger Hofwagen, in diesem die beiden Obersthofmeister:

S. E. Graf Ignaz Van der Straten-Penthoz
Graf Yve de Baray.

Der sechsspännige zweisitzige Wagen des k. k. Oberststallmeisters Sr. Ex. des Fürsten zu Thurn und Taxis von Stallofficieren zu Pferde umgeben.

Eine Abtheilung der k. k. Leibgarde-Reiter-Escadron zu Pferde.

Eine Trabantengarde-Abtheilung mit den Fahnen und klingendem Spiele.

Der mit sechs Schimmeln bespannte Prachtwagen, in welchem links Ihre Maj. die **Königin von Belgien** und rechts die Frau **Prinzessin Stephanie** sitzt.

Zur linken Seite des Wagens reitet der commandirende FZM. Freih. v. Philippovic mit gesenktem Säbel.

Zur rechten Seite des Wagens geht der k. k. Equipagen-Inspector, an jedem Wagenschlag zwei k. k. Leib-Lakaien, sechs Trabanten-Leibgarde, sechs Leibegarde-Reiter mit ihren Chargen.

Sechs k. k. Edelknaben zu Pferde.

Eine Abtheilung der k. k. Arcieren-Leibgarde zu Pferde.

Eine Abtheilung der k. ungarischen Leibgarde zu Pferde mit Pantherfellen und Csismen.

Ein sechsspänniger zweisitziger Hofwagen, in diesem die beiden Obersthofmeisterinnen:

J. E. Gräfin de Jonghe d'Ardoye
J. E. Gräfin Caroline Henricourt de Grünne.

Zwei sechsspännige viersitzige Hofwagen mit je drei Palast-damen und zwar:

J. D. Fürstin Auersperg-Kinsky
J. D. Fürstin Fürstenberg-Khevenhüller
Frau Gräfin Hardegg-Harnoncourt.

J. E. Gräfin Taaffe-Csaky
J. E. Gräfin Mannsfeld-Festetics
Frau Gräfin Pallavicini-Szechenyi.

Eine Compagnie des Infanterie-Regimentes Freiherr von Mollinary Nr. 38 und eine Escadron des Dragoner-Regimentes Carl Prinz von Preußen Nr. 8.

Left: The Order of Procession for the ceremonial
arrival of Princess Stephanie of Belgium · 1881
The official reception of the bride began on the
Karlsplatz · The names of the Austrian aristocracy
attest their varied European origin and reflect the
supranational character of the Austrian Empire
Photographer unknown

"The Ceremonial Arrival of Her Imp. Highness the Most Serene Lady
Princess Stephanie of Belgium as Bride to His Imperial and Royal
Highness the Most Serene Crown Prince and Archduke Rudolph
in Vienna on Monday, May 9, 1881, at one o'clock in the afternoon."

Right: The Viennese greet the Emperor · About 1896
Photographer unknown
Below: Carriages arriving at St Stephen's Cathedral for the
service to celebrate the Emperor's birthday · About 1896
Photo: Beer, Klagenfurt

Right: A squadron of the Life Guards on the way to its barracks · On the right can be seen the Parliament, in the background the Town Hall · About 1900 · Photographer unknown

Below: Ringstrasse and Opera · About 1900 · The sidelanes of the Ring were reserved for those on horseback Photographer unknown

Page 88: Advertisement pillar in a suburb · About 1899 Photographer unknown

Page 89: Stephansplatz · About 1900 · Photo: Beer, Klagenfurt

Right: Iglauer wet-nurses · 1906 · They were fostermothers to whole generations of upper class infants · Photo: E. Mayer
Below: "Buy Ladles!" Slovak pedlars offering hand-carved wooden wares · About 1894
Photo: Pichler, Vienna

625 1996   Buchanan

Wed   Fri

    Thursday   WMUR Debate

    Sat.   Yokens   3pm
    Sun 1   Crown Plaza Nashua
              2 sommersett Blvd.

Alexander   626 5296
    Thurs. nite pre debate rally   6:30

Forbes   628 1996
    Thurs.
    Sat. 10AM D. Webster College

Galician Orthodox Jews on the
Karmeliterplatz in the Leopoldstadt
(II. District) · About 1915 · Photo:
Pichler, Vienna

Woman selling lemons
on the Landstrasser Hauptstrasse
1916 · Photo: Pichler, Vienna

92

Bosnian infantry, Schottentor · About 1900 · Photographer unknown

Hungarian Life Guards outside the Hofburg after the Changing of the Guard · About 1900 · Photo: Beer, Klagenfurt

Haberdashery pedlar on Am Hof · 1915 · Photo: Pichler, Vienna

The corner of Ringstrasse and Akademiestrasse
About 1915 · Photo: Pichler, Vienna

On the Graben, one of the smartest streets of Vienna
About 1916 · Photo: Pichler, Vienna

Right: Viennese housewife on the Naschmarkt · About 1905 · Photo: Pichler, Vienna

Left: Wiener Neustadt, arrival of the morning train from Vienna · About 1898 · The engine was probably built in 1865 · Photo: Pichler, Vienna
Below: Horse-drawn streetcar, with open-air upper deck, on the Schwarzenbergplatz · 1896 · Photographer unknown

Right: Café with billiard-table in Rudolfsheim
(XIV. District) · On the right, the cashier · Photographer
unknown
Below: Office interior · About 1885 · Magnesium flashlight
Photo: J. Löwy, Vienna

Top: Refuse removal before the First World
War · 1908 · Photo: E. Mayer, Vienna
Right: The Danube canal, near the Rossauer
Lände · The tenement houses, built to house the
working classes, dominate the landscape
About 1895 · Photographer unknown
Below: The Dogcart, the tradesman's vehicle
About 1900 · Photographer unknown

Right: Lichtenwerd, steam-driven streetcar · 1896
Photographer unknown
Below: Working girls in Breitensee (XIV. District)
Photo: Pichler, Vienna
Page 104/105: Navvies at the Philadelphia bridge
(XII. District) · About 1905 · Photo: Schuhmann

Right: Barge with a load of logs, on the Danube canal near the Brigitta bridge 1896 · A major portion of Vienna's supplies arrived by water · Photographer unknown
Below: An innkeeper with his guests in the Schleifmühlgasse, Wieden (IV. District) · 1899 · Photo: Stauda
Page 110: View from the giant Ferris Wheel down on to a terrifying throng of cabs and people at the entrance to the Prater · 1900 Photographer unknown

The garden of a Prater restaurant · 1906 · Photo: E. Mayer

Head waiter of the Prater restaurant Prohaska at the garden door · 1906 · Photo: E. Mayer

Right: Flower parade in the
Prater-Hauptallee · 1900
Photographer unknown
Below: Schoolboys in the
Prater-Hauptallee · About 1907
Photo: E. Mayer

The Praterstern on a Sunday · 1905 · Photographer unknown

Military band in "Café No. 3" in the Prater · 1896 · Photographer unknown

Right: In the Prater-Hauptallee · 1908 · Photo: E. Mayer

114

Left: "Living Photography"
"Everything Previous Surpassed"
"The American Biograph"
"Sensational Novelty"
Announcement of one of the first film
shows in the Prater · About 1900
Photo: Beer, Klagenfurt

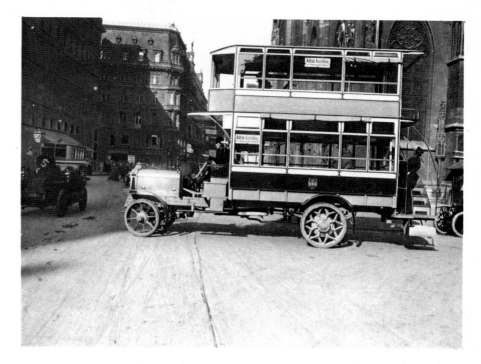

Double-decker bus from the Stephansplatz to the Adriatic
Exhibition in the Prater · 1913 · Photographer unknown

Bus stop, Stephansplatz · About 1912 · Photographer unknown

117

Vienna soon became the Mecca of the well-dressed woman · The fertile imagination of the Secession Movement in the arts soon found expression in textiles · Gustav Klimt and Kolo Moser designed dresses like these for the couture house of Flöge · But the really pioneering work came from the Vienna Workshops, the centre of the new artistic movement (see facing page) · Photos: D'Ora (p. 118) and photographer unknown (p. 119)

"The First Austrian Aeronautics Week, October 1911 · Setting off on the cross-country
flight Wiener Neustadt—Neunkirchen—Vienna—Wiener Neustadt, more than
112 Kilometres. In the cockpit, Lieutenant Bier, with Herr Baboucek and Frl. Steinschneider
as passengers · Next to the machine, Director Porsche" · Photo: Zapletal

120

SOCIETY

The social calendar of Court and aristocracy was as complicated as a railway timetable. It was important to be seen in the right places, vital for a man to ride, hunt, and shoot superbly well. For the society lady the pursuit of pleasure and elegance could become an arduous labour. The rhythm of life was prescribed: one went to the Derby at Freudenau and the Flower Parade in the Prater-Hauptallee. It was correct to watch the steeple-chasing at Pardubitz, or the Spring parade on the Schmelz, the Imperial parade ground on the outskirts of Vienna. There were seasons for visiting Karlsbad, for travelling to Nice and Paris, or for spending the summer "en famille" on the Adriatic. There were fixed points in this well-ordered world: the Hotel Sacher, where men-about-town entertained women not their wives, the *k. u. k.* Court Confectioner Demel where elegant ladies conversed politely over coffee and cakes. But life was not all pleasure: there were charity bazaars and concerts, visits to the sick and needy, and the dreary duties of the estates. It was an international society, comprising great families with their origins in Artois, Burgundy, and Flanders, from the Netherlands, Italy, Spain, from the Baltic, from Ireland, and of course, from Germany. From the bottom to the very top, the Dual Monarchy was a mixture of nationalities.

Portraits of two Viennese ladies
About 1865
Photographer unknown

Page 123: Members of the aristocracy
attending an aviation display at Aspern,
near Vienna · 1905 · Photo: Fachet, Vienna

Empress Elisabeth of Austria with her favourite dog "Shadow" · 1867 · The wife of the Emperor
Francis Joseph, she spent much of the later part of her life in ceaseless travelling · She was a
passionate huntswoman and followed the hounds in England and Ireland · The only part of the
Habsburg monarchy for which she had real affection was Hungary · She died tragically, by an
assassin's hand, on the shores of Lake Geneva in 1898 · Photo: Rabending

Above: Hungarian bodyguard of Baron Gerliczy
About 1908 · Photo: Kosel
Left: A house-concert by members of the aristocracy
in a Viennese palace · 1910 · Photo: Fachet, Vienna

Viennese society lady,
escorted by a Guards
officer, on the Freudenau
race-course at Vienna
About 1910
Photographer unknown

Countess Schönborn, July 9, 1912
Photo: D'Ora

130

131   Prague, racing at Kuchelbad · 1907 · Members of the aristocracy
in a characteristic mood · Photographer unknown

Three snapshots of the Freudenau race-course, Vienna · 1902 · Photographer unknown

Vienna, Neuer Markt · 1906 · Photo: E. Mayer, Vienna

Above: Aristocratic lady, with child, at her country-seat in Bohemia · In the background, the nanny Hanuška About 1905 · Photographer unknown
Left: Aristocratic ladies on a country walk at Friedau, Bohemia · About 1905 Photographer unknown

Isabella, Countess
Esterházy y Galánta · 1911
Photo: Kosel

Right: Past the winning-post at Freudenau · 1908
Photographer unknown

Right: Ilona Palmay, the Hungarian soubrette at Viennese theatres
1905 · For her the world of musical comedy turned into reality—
she married a Count Kinsky · Photographer unknown

Frau Schubart-Stern,
a member of Viennese
society · 1911
Photo: D'Ora

Informal family picture of the wedding of the Heir
Apparent, Archduke Francis Ferdinand, and Countess
Chotek in Reichstadt on July 1, 1900 · Photo: Carl,
Count Chotek

Page 140/141: Wedding of one of the
seven daughters of Count Clam-Gallas
in the Votivkirche, April 28, 1914 · Left,
the parents of the bride · Right, the groom,
Prince Auersperg, greeting the bride
Photographer unknown
Left: Golden Wedding celebration of Prince
Adolf and Princess Ida Schwarzenberg
at Frauenberg, Bohemia · 1907
Photographer unknown

Right: The launching of the *Viribus Unitis*, Trieste, June 24, 1911 · On the V.I.P. stand, the Heir Apparent and his wife · Photo: Fachet
Below: Military celebration in an Austrian garrison town · About 1905 · The garrison commander, on horseback, and the ladies of local society · Photographer unknown

Vienna, Freudenau race-course · 1901 · Photographer unknown

145   Officers of the Pardubitz garrison, with their pack, at the start of a hunt · 1904 · Photo: Pirker, Pardubitz

Officers' party in the Sacher garden in the Prater · About 1900 · Photographer unknown

Frau Anna Sacher · She was the proprietress of perhaps the most famous hotel in Vienna In its rooms the rich and noble debauched and even archdukes enjoyed the earthier pleasures of life · The name of Sacher acquired world renown because of a rich chocolate cake which was its speciality · 1907 · Photo: Kosel

An actress of the Deutsche Volkstheater, Vienna · About 1905
Photographer unknown

147

An actress of the Carltheater, Vienna
Photographer unknown

Above: Society at a launching, Trieste · 1910 · Photo: Goëss
Right: Unveiling of a statue of Emperor Francis Joseph as a huntsman, Bad Ischl,
August 24, 1910 · Photo: Schuhmann

The Vienna skating-rink
About 1905
Photographer unknown
Below: Horsemen in the Prater
during a Prater-Hauptallee social
parade · About 1901
Photographer unknown

Lady at the wheel · 1910 · Photographer unknown

Above: Ladies of high society on the race-course at Prague · 1906 · "Society" is already
equipped with cameras · Photographer unknown
Right: Emperor Francis Joseph with his great-nephew, who became Emperor Charles I
in 1916, at Mentone · 1894 · Private photo

Archduke Albrecht in old age, riding in an
"Electromobile" · The victor of Custozza in
1866, he was the doyen of the House of
Habsburg; the Emperor Francis Joseph relied
heavily on his advice · Photo: Fachet

The Imperial villa at Bad Ischl · The Emperor's summer-seat became
also that of the musical comedy monarchs Franz Lehár, Oscar
Straus and Leo Fall · To have been at Ischl at the right time and
the right place was a social "must" · Photo: Baldi-Würthle

Page 155 to 159: Members of the dynasty pay homage to the Emperor Francis Joseph at Ischl on his eightieth birthday, August 18, 1910 · Vehicle arrivals
Photo: Schuhmann
Page 156/157: Archduke Rainer in his carriage
Page 159: Archduke Eugene in his car
Page 160: Car of the Heir Apparent, Archduke Francis Ferdinand · Photo: Fachet

PRAGUE

The Holy Roman Emperor Charles V ruled over a realm on which the sun did not set and which stretched from the Carpathians via Spain and the Netherlands to the New World. When in 1521 he divided this empire, the hereditary Austrian lands were allocated to his brother Ferdinand.

Ferdinand, the first distinctly Austrian Habsburg, died in 1564. His unobtrusive sarcophagus in the centre of the choir of St Vitus's Cathedral in Prague is shared by his Jagellon wife Anna, marriage with whom brought him Bohemia and Hungary, and his son Maximilian II. The latter's son, Rudolf II, made Prague's citadel, the Hradčany, his main residence. As early as April 7, 1348, the Emperor Charles IV had founded in this city the first German-language university. In 1618 the Thirty Years War ensued on the Defenestration of Prague. And Prague was the birth-place of a whole string of Austria's outstanding twentieth century authors: Max Brod, Franz Kafka, Rainer Maria Rilke, Johannes Urzidil, Franz Werfel.

A special attribute was "Prague German", with that of the Kleinseite, or Lesser Town, as a sub-division of the species. As Urzidil wrote in *The Lost Beloved*, "Although Czech by birth, Herr Kubat had a thoroughly fluent command of German. He was from the Prague Kleinseite where so-called Kleinseite German was the second vernacular. People also called it savings bank German because most of the Bohemian Savings Bank's employees used it. This German . . . was a supranational German and as such symbolic of the consolidatory ethnic character of the Austro-Hungarian Monarchy."

Above: Vysherad · 1870 · According to tradition, this was the site where Princess Libussa, a great heroine of Bohemian history, had her residence · During the nineteenth century a Czech national cemetery was placed in the grounds of the earlier fortress · Among those buried there are Smetana and Dvořák · Photo: F. Fridrich

Right: The Hradčany · 1870 This is an unusual view which shows St Vitus's Cathedral before its completion · In the fourteenth century the Hussite Wars had meant the interruption of its construction and until 1873 only the choir and tower were standing · On the occasion of the millenary celebrations of St Wenceslas (1929), the building was at last completed · 1876 Photo: F. Fridrich

Page 163, above: Lesser Town (Kleinseite) with the Hradčany and Charles Bridge · 1860 Photo: W. Rupp

Page 163, below: The former Rossmarkt (horse market), now the Wenceslas Square, seen from the Rosstor where today the National Museum stands · 1876 · Photo: F. Fridrich

166

Above: The steamer *Prag* before its maiden voyage on the Vltava (Moldau) · 1865
Photo: J. Eckert
Left above: F. Fridrich, Court Photographer · 1865
Left below: A Prague woman · 1845 · Daguerreotype · Photographer unknown—A Prague
couple · 1867 · Photo: A. Helm

Above: Approach to the Neutor (new gate) from the city · 1874 · Prague's fortifications were demolished somewhat later than those of Vienna · Photo: K. Pták
Right: St James's church fair in front of the Ujezd Gate · About 1880 · In the background, the Hungermauer (famine wall) and the Hradčany · Photo: K. Maloch

The Powder Tower, with the old pyramidal roof · 1865 · Photographer unknown

The Graben · 1869 · This was the traditional Sunday walk of Prague's German population; Czechs took their stroll in the Nationalstrasse on the other side of Wenceslas Square · Photo: Beer

Above: Radetzky monument on the Lesser Town Ring · 1870 · In the background, the "Caffé-Salon zum Marschall Radetzky" which continues as a café today · The monument was removed in 1919 · Photographer unknown
Left: Funeral of Field Marshal Alfred, Prince Windischgrätz who had died on March 21, 1862, at Vienna · The scene is at the Zollamt (customs house) · The Field Marshal had in June 1848 put down the uprising in Prague and in October of the same year captured Vienna
Photo: Horn, Prague

173

Above: Commander and grenadier of the Prague city militia · About 1868
Photographer unknown
Right: Visit of Emperor Francis Joseph · 1874 · Festive decorations on the former Rossmarkt (horse
market), now the Wenceslas Square · Photo: K. Pták

Above: Illumination of the National Theatre on the occasion of the opening of the Francis Bridge
1901 · Photographer unknown
Right: Triumphal arch, on the occasion of the Emperor's visit, with the inscription "God Bring
Him Luck" · 1874 · Photographer unknown

177

Triumphal column outside the
Ujezd Gate on the occasion of the
Emperor's visit · 1866
Photographer unknown

Above: Villa Bertramka in Smichov · About 1890 · Here, in 1787, Mozart composed the overture to *Don Giovanni* Smichov, once known as "the smiling meadow" and dotted with rococo palaces, was overrun by factories and tenements during the nineteenth century · Photographer unknown

Right: The Francis Bridge and National Theatre · 1910 Photographer unknown

Left: The Nostitz Theatre · Here, on October 29, 1787, the original performance of Mozart's *Don Giovanni* took place Photographer unknown

KOVOVÉ ZBOŽÍ A NÁSTROJE.
Domácí a kuchyňské nářadí.
KAREL LÜFTNER
CARL
Haus- u. Küchengeräthe.
METALLWAREN u. WERKZEUGE.

182

Wenceslas Square and the National Museum · In addition to the horse-drawn streetcar, there is already an electric streetcar
Photographer unknown

Gendarme on horseback under the "Bruska" · Photographer unknown

183

Above: Restaurant "Na Svinčíku" (The Piglet) · Photographer unknown
Right: Prague women · About 1900 · Photographer unknown

Carrying away the "Beer Corpses" · Victims of the world-famous Bohemian beer were brought home, free of charge, in a hearse-like basket with a special "gun crew" · Photographer unknown

Above: Second-hand shop in the Jewish quarter · Photographer unknown
Right above: The old ghetto · The old synagogue, dating from the thirteenth century, and
the Jewish Town Hall with its two famous clocks · The face of one has Hebrew characters and
its hands move from right to left · Photographer unknown

186

The "Flying Café"
About 1905
Photographer unknown

On the Prague race-course Kuchelbad · Princess Johanna Rohan (in white dress), Prince
Zdenko Lobkowitz, Archduchess Maria Annunziata, Prince Georg Christian ("Gox")
Lobkowitz · Photographer unknown

BUDAPEST

Budapest, capital of the Hungarian half of the Empire, has preserved hardly any important reminders of its past. Because Buda's Castle Hill, a fortified precinct for more than a thousand years, continually changed hands, the constant fighting over the site meant that barely one stone remained upon another. The Turks held it for nearly a hundred and fifty years, but a few baths are the sole traces of their occupation. In 1872 the two localities on either side of the Danube, Buda (called Ofen in German) and Pest, were officially merged and, with Alt-Ofen added for good measure, became a single city.

The Hungarians' exuberant patriotism and their endeavours to outdo Vienna were the inspiration behind the array of buildings erected on the occasion of the celebrations to mark the millennium of the Magyar conquest of the country. What had been no more than a dreary Danube landing-spot was transformed into the ground on which stood Europe's largest Houses of Parliament, London excepted. The little wood on the edge of the town was felled to make room for the Millennium Monument. The fortifications of Castle Hill were planed into the candy-floss architecture of the Fisher Bastion. The Romanesque tower of St Matthew's, coronation church of Hungarian kings, was Gothicized. The elegant exteriors in the centre of Pest adhered faithfully to *fin de siècle* style. In 1892, on the twenty-fifth anniversary of Francis Joseph's coronation as King of Hungary, Budapest was endowed with the title "Capital and Residence".

On December 30, 1916, Castle Hill witnessed the last coronation of a King of Hungary, that of Charles, last Emperor of Austria.

Above: Fruit market and landing-place on the Pest embankment, opposite the Royal Palace
About 1885—1890 · Photographer unknown
Page 192: A Budapest family · About 1860 · Photo: Janos Tiedge
Page 193: The "Water Town", the oldest part of Buda · Castle Hill, with the Church of
St Matthew, the coronation church of Hungary's monarchs, stands over it · About 1860
The view shows the church in its original condition before it was gothicized in 1874
Photo: Heidenhaus

Right: The famous suspension bridge, from the Pest side
About 1898 · Designed by William Clark and built by Adam Clark,
1842—1849, it was the first bridge to join Buda and Pest
Photo: Pichler, Vienna
Below: Open-air carriage of the Pest municipal horse-drawn
streetcar · About 1866—1870 · Photo: Klösz
Page 196/197: View of the Danube and Royal Palace from the
customs house · About 1896 · Photo: Beer
Page 198: Flower-sellers and porter on the Museum Ring
About 1900 · Photographer unknown
Page 199: Hungarian peasant at the weekly market
Photo: E. Wellisz

Above: Armin Martonfalvy · 1893 · Photo: J. Fodor
Left: Andrássy-ut, Budapest's main shopping street
About 1896 · Photo: Erdelyi
Below: A rich Budapest couple with servant
Photographer unknown

Above: Last excursion of the so-called "Imperial Coach" on the occasion of the coronation of the Emperor Charles as King of Hungary at Buda, December 30, 1916 · In the coach, Empress Zita and the little Crown Prince Otto (Dr. Otto Habsburg) · Photo: Army Photographic Department
Right: Countess Zichy in her robes for the coronation ceremony · Photo: D'Ora

Hungarian Guards accompanying the royal coach · Photo: Army Photographic Department

Left: Hungarian magnates on the way to the coronation · Photographer unknown

Above: The last session in the old Town Hall, February 8, 1900 · Photographer unknown
Right: The telephone exchange · 1897 · Photographer unknown
Page 207: Pavilion of the Oetl Machine Factory at the Hungarian National Fair · 1885 · Photographer unknown

Arrival at a Budapest railway station · About 1910 · Photo: Erdelyi

Shoeshine · Photo: Erdelyi

Above: Cabs waiting in front of the Royal Palace · Photo: Erdelyi
Page 210 above: Church fête on Szent-Gellért hill · In the background, the Danube
Photographer unknown
Below: Eating-house, with gipsy band, in the Francis Town district · Photographer unknown

AGRAM

The thousand year old capital of the former Kingdom of Croatia, with its historic nucleus, is situated on two hills separated by a shallow valley. The whole is now called Zagreb and the contemporary name for the hilly parts, which during the Middle Ages waged fierce warfare against each other, are Kaptol and Gornji-Grad (Upper Town). St Mark's and the Stone Gate in Gornji-Grad and the Archbishop's Palace and the Cathedral of St Stephen in Kaptol are among the monuments. During the major earthquake in 1880 the Cathedral steeple—still to be seen in its original state on page 213—collapsed and was re-erected in Gothic style.

The Croats were among the Habsburgs' most devoted supporters. They were to be met on every field of battle alongside the *Granitscharen*—the "frontier hordes", the name given to the troops from the Military Frontier area established against the Turks in 1522. For Croat officers it was a matter of social prestige that, ennobled for valour, they should choose German titles. The results are to be seen, for example, in the 1841 Army List which records the following officers as belonging to the First Wallachian Regiment of the Imperial-Royal Frontier Infantry: Captain Franz Markesich von Kaisershuld ("Imperial Favour"), Lieutenant Secsujacz von Heldenfeld ("Heroes Field"), and Lieutenant Sabatovics von Kronentreu ("Loyal to the Crown"). Incidentally, this regiment's uniform lapels were known as *paperlgrün* ("parrotty green"). The Senior Naval Command at Venice numbered among its officers Frigate Commander Johann Buratovich von Flaggentreu ("Loyal to the Flag"), Lieutenant Franz Rubessa von Mastenwald ("Forest of Masts"), and Lieutenant Ivanosich von Küstenfeld ("Coastal Field"). After 1848 these *Biedermeier* names—reminiscent of the Austrian satirist Herzmanovsky-Orlando—disappeared and nationalism induced Croat officers too to select Slav titles. To blame also was the Compromise with Hungary which once again subjected Croatia—the kingdom with the Habsburg dynasty's most loyal followers—to Magyar sovereignty.

Above: The Stone Gate, Upper Town · About 1864 · Photo: Schwoiser

Page 213: A monument was raised to Governor Jellačić, "Habsburg's Saviour", for his part in the overthrow of the revolutions in Vienna and Hungary · The inscription reads "Ban Jellačić 1848"
Photo: Beer · 1896

Page 214: Ivan Kukuljević, father of the Illyrian Movement · 1861 · Historian and Croat patriot, he was the first member of the Sabor, the Croat Parliament, to speak there in that language · Photo: Hühn

Page 215: Agram in 1870 · Photo: Ivan Standl

216

Petar von Preradović, Croatia's greatest poet and an Austrian general · Away from home for many years, he first wrote in German, but during a longer stay in Dalmatia he rediscovered the excellences of his native tongue and his patriotism · Thenceforward (1842) his writings and his compositions were in Croat · His ballad *The Wanderer* is the most eloquent expression in verse of the spirit of the Illyrian Movement
Photo: Pommer · 1856

Jellačić Square · 1894 · Photo: Ivan Standl

Above: Triumphal gateway at the junction of Ilica und Jellačić Square on the occasion of the visit by Crown Prince Rudolph and his wife, Crown Princess Stephanie, on June 10, 1888 · Within months he was dead by his own hand at Mayerling, found with the body of his mistress, Baroness Marie Vetsera
Photographer unknown
Page 220: Laying the coping-stone of the New Theatre, October 14, 1895 · Emperor Francis Joseph thanks the crowd from the balcony for its ovations · Photo: Mosinger-Breyer
Page 221 above: Wedding of Mary Adrowski, a well-known member of local society · 1909
Photo: Mosinger-Breyer
Below: (a) Count Rudi Norman, an important landowner, in Croat Magnate's uniform
1900 · Photo: Winter, Vienna · (b) Ljerka Šram, actress at the Croat National Theatre · About 1898
Photo: Mosinger-Breyer

221

Trakošćan Castle, property of the Draskovich family, near Agram · About 1870 · Photo: Standl

Miss Stankovica, better known as Sofija von Hatz · 1879 · Photo: Fickert

The "Sokols", or Hawks, were a patriotic Slav gymnastic association · Under the guise of healthy exercise, these
cyclists planned political activity · 1887 · Photographer unknown

CRACOW

Included among the many titles borne by the Emperor of Austria were those of King of Galicia and Lodomeria, Grand Duke of Cracow, and Duke of Auschwitz and Zator.

Galicia still has a familiar ring in modern ears, but Lodomeria will sound strange to most. It comes from the former principality of Vlodimir, just as Galicia does from the name Halicz. Auschwitz and Zator were Upper Silesian dukedoms, and all four of these domains accrued to Austria in 1772 on the occasion of the first partition of Poland. Only in 1795 did Cracow, under the third partition of Poland, fall into Austria's lap. The Congress of Vienna turned the city into a Free State, but in 1846 it was again incorporated into the Empire as a grand duchy.

From the early days of the Middle Ages until the seventeenth century Cracow retained the status of a capital. Poland's kings were crowned and buried in the cathedral beside the castle on the historic Wawel Hill. The mediaeval ground-plan of the city, with its Market Place and famous cloth halls, survives. But of its mighty battlements, mostly razed at the beginning of the nineteenth century, there only remain the Barbican, the Florian Gate, and the Joiners', Carpenters' and Lace-Makers' Bastions. The city's defence lay in the hands of the guilds who recruited their own militias and annually held a competition to test their readiness for a call to arms. In 1565 King Sigismund Augustus donated the famous "Cock o' the Walk", a silver effigy of a cock, as a prize for the victor in this contest.

The "Polish Club", the collective description for the Polish delegates to the *Reichsrat*, the Parliament at Vienna, played a special part in political life, not wholly unlike that of the Irish M.P.s at Westminster during the latter half of the nineteenth century. Old photographs testify to the fact that nationalist demonstrations, such as that of the Polish victory over the Teutonic Knights or the unveiling of a monument to Tadeusz Kosciuszko, hero of the struggle for national unity, were a common occurrence.

226

227

Right: Cracow from the west, seen from Kosciuszko Hill, at the end of the nineteenth century · Photo: Krieger
Page 227: The Church of Our Lady · About 1865 · Inside is an altar by Veit Stoss, one of the most famous woodcarvers of Gothic times · Today still, as for many centuries past, at each hour a bugle-call suddenly reverberates in all directions from the top of the tower and recalls to mind that thirteenth century trumpeter who, in the midst of sounding this signal, was struck down mortally by a Mongol arrow · Photographer unknown

Wawel Hill · About 1880 · For centuries the castle was the residence and the cathedral
the coronation and burial church of Polish kings · Photo: Krieger

Fifth centenary celebration of the victory by the Poles over the Teutonic Knights at
Grunwald near Tannenberg, August 15—17, 1910 · Photographer unknown

Right: Inhabitants of Kazimierz, the
Jewish quarter · 1865 · Photo: Krieger

Rabbis · 1865 · Photo: Krieger

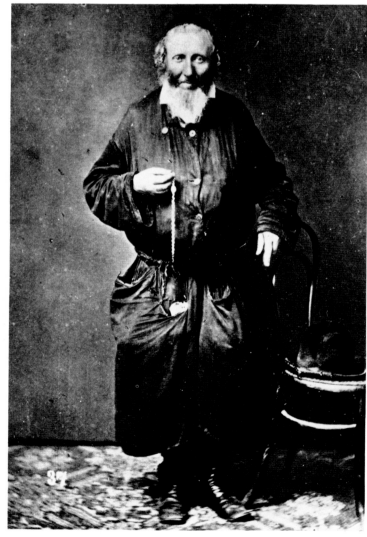

234

Shops in the Ulica Krakowska, Kazimierz · 1900 · Photo: Krieger

The Old Synagogue in Kazimierz, end of the nineteenth century · Photo: Krieger

Unveiling of the Tadeusz Kosciuszko monument on the Ringplatz,
March 24, 1894 · It stood on the spot where a century earlier the national
hero had sworn his oath to fight against the powers occupying his country—
Prussia, Russia and Austria · Photographer unknown

236

The barbican in front of the last remnants of the mediaeval fortifications, the
Floriani Tower and a few battlements · About 1900 · Photographer unknown

The Sharpshooters club on the occasion of
the "Enthronement" of the "Cock o' The
Walk" · 1914 · Photographer unknown

The champion shot ("Cock o' The Walk"),
with the famous silver cock · This, the work
of a Cracow Renaissance goldsmith, was a
present made in 1565 to the Cracow
Sharpshooters Fellowship by King Sigismund
Augustus, last of the Jagellon family on the
Polish throne · Photographer unknown

THE PROVINCES

Aussig (in northern Bohemia), Brody (now in Russia), and Cattaro (today's Kotor, the Adriatic tip of Jugoslavia bordering on Albania) constituted the westernmost, easternmost and southernmost points of the triangle which contained the colourful medley of territories, peoples and cities constituting an empire of fifty-one million inhabitants, the "Kingdoms and *Länder* represented in the *Reichsrat*" and the "Lands of the Crown of St Stephen", its Austrian and Hungarian halves respectively. Individual units were Lower Austria, Upper Austria, Salzburg, Styria, Carinthia, Krain, the Littoral, Tirol and Vorarlberg, Bohemia, Moravia, Silesia, Galicia and Lodomeria, the Bukovina, Dalmatia, Hungary, Transylvania, Fiume, Croatia, Slavonia, Bosnia and Hercegovina.

Besides 12 million Germans it was composed of
- 10 million Hungarians
- 6.6 million Czechs
- 2 million Slovaks
- 5 million Poles
- 4 million Ruthenes
- 3.2 million Croats
- 2 million Serbs
- 2.9 million Roumanians
- 1.4 million Slovenes
- 0.8 million Italians
- 0.6 million Islamic Slavs
- 0.5 million Others

It was a small-scale United Europe held together by the superstructure of the Monarchy.

Above: Snapshot of a train arriving in Liesing station, Lower Austria · 1882 · Photo: Kroh
Page 241: Graz, the Herrengasse · About 1874 · Graz, the Dual Monarchy's retirement Mecca,
was especially favoured for this purpose by those no longer on the army's active list
Photo: Burger, Vienna

Linz, Danube landing-place · About 1905 · Photographer unknown

Above: Mountain peasant family in Goldegg, near Salzburg, with their farm-hands
About 1900 · The hands, male and female alike, were given names (such as "cartwright") which
corresponded to their occupation · Photographer unknown
Page 245 above: March-past in Innsbruck of the Tirolese Sharpshooters' Associations · 1909
The occasion was the centenary celebration of the liberation struggle against the French
Photographer unknown
Page 245 below: Salzburg · 1862 · View from the Kapuzinerberg towards Schloss Mirabell and
the bastions, at that date still standing · Photo: Baldi und Würthle
Page 246/247: Gmunden (Salzkammergut), Lake Promenade · 1870 · Photo: Burger, Vienna

Franzensbad, Bohemia, the Kaiserstrasse
About 1860 · Photo: Fridrich

Karlsbad, the "Hall of Friendship"
About 1870
Photographer unknown

AUSGANG
KREUZBRUNNEN

Page 248 left below: Karlsbad, the town-drummer
About 1860 · Such a drummer was used at that date
in many small towns and villages to proclaim official
announcements · Photo: Winkelmann, Teplitz

Marienbad, Promenade · 1900 · Photo: Fridrich

Right: Karlsbad, visitors with the indispensable beaker for taking the waters · 1895 · Photo: Beer
Below: Karlsbad, the *Alte Wiese,* the street which was one of the resort's focal points · 1910
Photo: Österreichische Lichtbildstelle · These three spas were probably the most famous in the
Dual Monarchy and they were internationally renowned as well · Franzensbad, whose
architecture breathed the spirit of the Classic Revival; Marienbad, the "Riviera without
a Beach", was the spa where monarchs enjoyed giving private dinner parties and ministers
liked to confer, while its place in literary history was ensured through Goethe's *Marienbader
Elegie;* and as for Karlsbad "the whole world" met there, starting with Wallenstein, including
Peter the Great of Russia, Goethe, Schiller, Chopin, Metternich and Bismarck, and working
up to the monarchs of finance at the turn of the twentieth century

Above: Unveiling of the monument to the Emperor Francis Joseph at Jägerndorf, Silesia, October 4, 1908 · The occasion was the celebration of the sixtieth anniversary of the Emperor's reign · Photographer unknown
Page 252—253: Brünn (Brno), Parade of the *k. u. k.* Infantry Regiment No. 49 · 1900 Brünn was (and remains) the capital of Moravia · Photographer unknown

Klattau, Bohemia, Dragoons deploy for the parade on the occasion of the Emperor's
birthday, August 18, 1906 · Photographer unknown

Jägerndorf, Silesia, consecration of the colours of the
Apprentices' Association · About 1855
Photographer unknown

Rožnau, a small Moravian town, the main square with
bandstand · About 1875 · Photographer unknown

257

Left: The steamship-station of Aussig on the Elbe, the main centre of Bohemian industry · 1905 · Photographer unknown
Below: Pressburg (Bratislava), the theatre · About 1870
Photo: Karl Körper, Pressburg
Page 258 below: Pressburg, from the Danube · About 1870
From 1526 to 1784 Pressburg was the capital of Hungary
Photo: Karl Körper, Pressburg
Page 260—261: The Pardubitz hunt, Autumn 1908
The garrison town of Pardubitz, in Bohemia,
was famous for its steeple-chase, the most
difficult in Europe, over 6,600 yards long and
with more than 30 hurdles which required
enormous leaps by horse and rider · Photo: Pirker

Pilsen (Plzeň), Bohemia, the weekly market · About 1905 · Pilsen was the site of both the
Bürgerliche Brauhaus, the Civic Brewery, opened in 1842 and the largest in Europe, and of
the Škoda Works, one of the Dual Monarchy's principal armament manufacturers
Photo: Pichler

Page 264/265: Hungarian peasant family in the neighbourhood of
Fünfkirchen (Pécs) · About 1890 · Photo: Zelesny, Pécs

Gipsy women in Orsova, on the Danube, in the region of the Iron Gates
About 1905 · Photo: Pichler

Stehli, East Galicia, peasant house · 1910
Photographer unknown

Rawa Ruska, East Galicia · A Jewish family · 1910
Photographer unknown

Rawa Ruska, market · 1910 · Photographer unknown

Turnpikes at the Austro-Russian border before the East Galician town of Brody · About 1905
Podwoloczyska, at that time famous and infamous alike as the frontier crossing-point for
diplomats and spies, lay a little farther to the south · Photo: Pichler

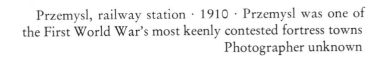

Przemysl, railway station · 1910 · Przemysl was one of
the First World War's most keenly contested fortress towns
Photographer unknown

269

East Galician roadside inn · 1905 · Photo: Pichler

Lemberg (Lvov), capital of Galicia, the theatre · 1908
Its architects, Helmer and Fellner, were responsible for
building nearly all provincial theatres, most of them on the
same pattern · Photo: Pichler

Left above: Roumanian peasant from Transylvania
Photo: Adler, Kronstadt
Left below: Ruthenians on the market square of
Czernowitz · 1897 · Photo: Goëss

The wife of the governor of the Bukovina at the weekly market in Czernowitz
1897 · Photo: Goëss

Ladies bathing at Grado, the largest seaside resort
in the Dual Monarchy · About 1898 · Photo: Beer

Grado, the Beach · About 1898 · Photo: Beer

Headquarters of the Austrian (later Austro-Hungarian) Lloyd shipping line on the Piazza Grande, Trieste, the Dual Monarchy's third largest city · 1897 · Austrian Lloyd was founded in 1836 and owned in 1913 a fleet of 62 ships comprising a total of 236,000 tons · Photo Beer

The Lloyd steamers *Baron Gautch*,
Metcovich and *Graf Wurmbrand*
beside the jetty at Trieste · 1910
Photographer unknown

Lloyd headquarters at the corner of Piazza Grande and Sanità, Trieste · 1897
Its architecture corresponds exactly to the historicism which characterizes the
Vienna Ringstrasse · Photo: Beer

Trieste, view of the harbour · 1888 · The city voluntarily
accepted Habsburg sovereignty in 1382
Photo: Giuseppe Wulz, Trieste

On board the Lloyd steamer *Baron Beck* · 1910 · Photo: Beer

Above: Fiume (Rijeka), the Town Hall tower · About 1905 · Photo: Pichler
Right: Abbazia (Opatija), Villa Angiolina, the property of Crown Prince Rudolph
Right above: View from the garden towards the sea · 1895

280

Zengg (Senj), the old castle Nehaj ("Fear Nought"), on the Dalmatian coast · 1896
Photo: Margetić

Below: The Glavizza Mosque near Mostar, capital of Hercegovina
1878 · Photo: Franz Laforest, Mostar
Right: Turkish *Han* (inn), near Kiseljak · 1878 · This was the year
in which Austria occupied Bosnia and Hercegovina, territories hitherto
under Turkish sovereignty · Both photos were taken during the
Austrian entry · Photo: I. Löwy, Vienna

Above: Sarajevo, soirée at the local government
headquarters, July 6, 1910 · Photographer unknown
Left: Sarajevo, card-game during a soirée, April 6,
1911 · Sarajevo was the capital of Bosnia
Photographer unknown

287   Sarajevo, the Turkish quarter, Čaršija · 1895 · Photo: Beer

Cattaro (Kotor), visit by the German battleships *Stosch, Charlotte, Moltke* and *Gneisenau*
to the most southerly point of the Austro-Hungarian Empire · About 1890
Photographer unknown

THE MILITARY

The Austro-Hungarian Monarchy was a state built around its army. The poet Grillparzer had written of the great Field Marshal Radetzky: "In your camp is Austria"; certainly this was how the Emperor Francis Joseph, his generals and officers saw their society. Theirs was a peacetime army which never fought a major campaign in almost half a century before 1914. It was dominated by its Court generals, its armchair administrators and the colourless officials of the Ministry of War. Despite the bright uniforms its officers usually lived dull routine lives in desolate garrisons far from the delights of Vienna or Budapest. The army, like the state it served, was a compromise. It was split into three, with the national defence forces of Hungary and Austria acting with virtual independence of the central military system. This recipe for chaos and inefficiency was fulfilled when war did come. The officers of the army and navy were a caste apart from the rest of society, for they had discarded their national identities when they put on their uniforms. To the twelve races of the Empire should be added a thirteenth: the officer corps, loyal and true to the Habsburg dynasty, even when the state had crumbled. They were the true "Imperialists" of the Habsburg Empire.

Krechor near Kolin, June 18, 1897 · Official guests at the unveiling of a monument to those
killed in action at the Battle of Kolin, June 18, 1757, where the Austrians defeated the Prussians
under Frederick the Great · Photographer unknown

Left: Emperor Francis Joseph's arrival at Banffy-Hunyad, near Klausenburg (Cluj), on September 26, 1895, after the end of the manoeuvres in Transylvania
Photographer unknown
Below: An officer of the Austro-Hungarian army
Photographer unknown

Leipzig ("Battle of the Nations") centenary celebration on the Schwarzenbergplatz, Vienna,
October 16, 1913 · After the parade in front of the monument to Prince Schwarzenberg,
commander of the Austrian forces at Leipzig, the troops marched down the Ringstrasse past
Emperor Francis Joseph who declined to set foot on the small Persian carpet prepared for him
The picture shows the leading file of the "Hoch- und Deutschmeister" Infantry Regiment
Photo: Schuhmann

Page 296: Leipzig centenary celebration, October 16, 1913 · The colours of a
Hungarian regiment are carried past · Photo: Schuhmann

Celebration by Infantry Regiment No. 4, "Hoch- und Deutschmeister", in Vienna · 1896
For special occasions elegant tents were always available for the Emperor and his *entourage*
Photo: Lechner

Centenary celebration of the Battle of Aspern (where Napoleon sustained a defeat at the hands
of the Archduke Charles), May 21, 1909 · No celebration was complete without the attendance
of a company of maids of honour and in this picture the Emperor is just being greeted by such
a group · Photographer unknown

Above: Leipzig centenary celebration · 1913 · March-past on the Ringstrasse of the City
of Vienna Regiments' contingent · Photo: Schuhmann
Right above: March-past of a Hungarian regiment · Photo: Schuhmann

298

A soldier of the emperor · When war came men like him fought with courage and surprising loyalty: the feared desertions "en masse" did not come · Photo: Schuhmann

Spring parade · 1896 · The parade, in which contingents from every arm of the service
participated, took place annually on the Schmelz, Vienna's enormous, dusty and stony
parade-ground · In this picture the Emperor can be seen returning the salute of the troops
with raised sword · His *entourage* follows · Photo: Lechner

Page 302: The 15th Dragoons · 1912 · The departure of a squadron from its home barracks at Traiskirchen for garrison duties at Zolkiev, Galicia · The inscription "Oils and Gas" on the wall in the background is a harbinger of the new age which will displace the horse as a means of transport · Photographer unknown

302

Above: On manoeuvres in Bohemia · Artillery
leaving Nepomuk · Photographer unknown
Right: Imperial manoeuvres in Southern
Moravia · 1909 · In the foreground, orderlies
resting · Right, standing, Count Paar, A.D.C.
to the Emperor · Photo: Fachet

Imperial manoeuvres in Carinthia · 1899 · At the close of these exercises Emperor Francis
Joseph drives to Ebenthal near Klagenfurt · Photo: Beer

Society ladies on the
umpire's stand during the
manoeuvres at Stekna,
Bohemia · 1905 · Photo:
Deport and Panzer, Prague

Right: International Naval Review off Gravosa, the harbour of Ragusa (Dubrovnik) · 1880 · Photographer unknown
Below: These pictures certainly reflect some of the romance which attached to the days of sail, but each of these ships was also fitted with screw-propulsion · On the left is the gunboat *Kerka* (crew, 100), launched at Venice in 1860 and condemned as unserviceable in 1908; on the right, the frigate *Laudon* (crew, 480), launched in 1873
Photo, about 1890 · Photographer unknown

Left: The Heir Apparent, Archduke Francis Ferdinand d'Este, at the launching of the battleship *Viribus Unitis*, Trieste June 24, 1911 · Photo: Fachet
Right: The launching of the *Viribus Unitis* from the Stabilimento Tecnico, Trieste · Photographer unknown
Below: Three ships of the *Viribus Unitis* class (dreadnoughts, an early twentieth century type of battleship) at Pola, the Dual Monarchy's main naval harbour · In the foreground, the *Szent Istvan;* behind, the rapid cruiser *Saida;* in the right-hand background, two ships of the *Archduke Charles* class
Photographer unknown

Left: "Us they've got!" Conscripts in a Vienna street · 1915 · A posy of flowers with oak leaves and coloured glass balls indicated that men had been found fit for service · Photo: Pichler
Above: The beginning of the end · Passers-by in a Budapest street read the poster carrying the Emperor's mobilization order, dated August 1, 1914: "To My Peoples!—It was my dearest wish to devote the years which God in His mercy may still grant me to working for peace and to protecting my peoples from the heavy sacrifices and burdens of war · Providence has seen fit to decide otherwise..." Photographer unknown

313

INDEX OF PHOTOGRAPHS

THE MILITARY